A DICTIONARY OF THOUGHT

A DICTIONARY OF
THOUGHT

From My Writings and From My Evenings

BY DAGOBERT D. RUNES

PHILOSOPHICAL LIBRARY · NEW YORK

Manufactured in the United States of America

A DICTIONARY OF THOUGHT

A

ABHORRENCE
The crime they abhor in generations gone, they overlook in their own, because its commission is veiled by a camouflage of contemporary civilization.

ABILITY
Is measured not by the greatness of the talent but by the purpose for which it is employed.

ABNORMAL
All great ideas and all great actors on the stage of history were abnormal. Was Beethoven normal? Or Michelangelo? Da Vinci, Socrates, or Mohammed?

They all went off the norm, driving themselves incessantly for what they thought was vital and essential. You may call them neurotics, if you wish. Surely their response to given impulses was undue, strikingly undue, in the eyes of living mediocrities.

The nights of the truly outstanding are inhabited by demons, idols and visions. But without their fantasies and dreams, a dull place the normal era would be.

Treat gently the abnormal; he may carry some subtle talent under the cloud of his peculiarities.

ABOLITIONISM
The white man took willingly the black man as burden, but hesitates to take him as friend.

ABSENCE
Makes a good seasoning but a poor staple.

❦❦

Absence increases fondness—and ends in forgetfulness.

THE ABSOLUTE
As far as morals are concerned, what matters is only our awareness that they are relative to time, place and government.

ACCEPTANCE
By hasty multitudes is a point against rather than for an ism.

ACCIDENTS
Man proposes—and a blind goddess disposes.

ACTIONS
Speak loud but sometimes a whisper is more welcome.

ADHERENCE
Preconceived notions are the hardest to give up.

ADJUSTMENT
The adjusted are so completely oriented within themselves that nothing can penetrate that wall of egocentricity except what they chew and digest.

ADMIRATION
Is a balm when known, an offense when shown.

❦❦

Who fails to admire will never love.

ADOLESCENCE
Neither infancy nor childhood, but adolescence is decisive in the making of man. The tastes, physical and mental, fostered in those days will determine the rest of the living years.

ADVENTURE

Nothing is more intriguing than the soul of a fellow man.

※※

Man will search for starlings in foreign lands and pay no heed to the lark at home.

※※

The greatest adventures are experienced in the soul of man, not across oceans or deserts.

ADVERSITY

Is God's helpmate and the Devil's handmaiden.

ADVICE

Is poor service indeed if given by those who lack sense of direction.

※※

Advice should be given by the example of the accomplished, not by one's own meager experience.

AFFECTATION

They act like characters in a book, only they read the wrong book.

AFFECTION

Affection is the only cure for a lonely soul.

AGE

Is but one step from youth. Let the flippant remember they may even fumble that one.

※※

Age is a time for work, since most of the pleasures of youth have guttered out.

※※

Man's true age lies in the life span ahead of him, not the span behind him.

※※

[3]

Age is no cause for veneration. An old crocodile is still a menace and an old crow sings not like a nightingale.

❦❦

Age is wasted on the tired. It is the most precious time of life.

❦❦

Wisdom grows with the years but not in a barren soul.

❦❦

Gray hair is a sign of age, not wisdom.

❦❦

Some days we are ten years older than on others.

❦❦

A fool gets more hardened with age, a wise man gentler.

❦❦

The greatest tragedy of old age is to live on into a generation without peers.

AGGRESSION

How quick the sand of life runs out, and even the wasting is made doleful by man's impatient eristics.

AGNOSTIC

A timid person attempting to hide his insecurity under a metaphysical cloak. He is gnostic about himself but agnostic about everything else.

AGRICULTURE

Is a profession, not a way of life.

AHIMSA

This, the Hindu principle of non-killing of cows and other animals, has led to the killing of hundreds of thousands of Indian Moslems who ignored it. How often a religious tenet so drifts away from the original spirit that it leads to its opposite.

ALCHEMY

Superstition of yesteryear is the science of today. What science of our time will be the superstition of tomorrow? Laugh not at yesterday; tomorrow may have the laugh on you.

ALCOHOLISM
Society's legitimatized drug addiction.

ALMS
Were the early expression of social consciousness. The man who refused alms then is the cynic of our era.

AMATEUR
It is by the quality of his mistakes that you recognize the amateur.

AMBITION
Is a mongrel seed. You never know what will come of it until it is too late: the tree of life or poison ivy.

Great ambition has sometimes destroyed the one it possessed, but raised mankind a step or two.

AMERICA
Was erected with material that the builders had rejected: adventurers, refugees, criminals, bonded persons, slaves, the hunted and the outcasts. Its glory is the nimbus that forever hazes about the down-trodden.

America has freed the world and the world cannot forgive her for that.

AMUSEMENT
Is the keyhole through which you can watch man unobserved.

ANCESTOR WORSHIP
May not only lead youth to search amid their heritage for the lasting values, but may tend to make older people prove their virtues by today's deeds.

ANCESTRY

Is something we all have, but an odd few insist upon it as their very own.

ANGELS

May be a figment of imagination, but devils are for real; I have met too many of them to doubt it.

❦❦

Angels are in the heavens, I am sure, because there are deeds done by mortals that are difficult to explain by the mortal nature of man. The angels of self-sacrifice and everlasting devotion, of courage and tenderness—they must be fluttering about in the winds high above, sometimes taking on the face of man and his flesh.

❦❦

Why did the Lord make so few winged ones and so many that crawl?

❦❦

I don't know if the angels have wings; I am sure the devils do, they move about so fast.

ANGER

Who never feels anger never cares.

❦❦

Anger is the big brother of compassion.

ANIMAL

A tiger may be ferocious but only man carries grudges from kin to kid.

❦❦

Man has succeeded in cowing almost every beast except his fellow man.

❦❦

Animals have no conscience. If they did, they would be better than people.

❦❦

Animals we all are, but they live for today, we for a to-morrow.

[6]

ANTICIPATION
Nothing really ever happens; anticipation is its own reward.

ANTIQUITY
They talk down its glory to flatter their own drabness.

APOLOGY
People will apologize for stepping on each other's toes, but not for crushing each other's hearts.

APPAREL
The drab tunic of the proletarian dictators is no less offensive a mockery of good taste than the gaudy uniforms of the sheiks of Araby.

APPARITIONS
Frighten us no more. No ghosts can match the horrible deeds of those this side the grave.

APPETITE
At the table of life some few forget in their hasty grab for wealth that shrouds have no pockets.

APPLAUSE
Plays the Siren on the ocean of life, sweet lips and subtle poison. Alexander, Attila, Hitler, Stalin—each sacrificed a generation on the altar of vanity.

Some can handle it and are stimulated—others just get drunk.

APPROVAL
By a fool is worse than rejection by a sage.

ARGUMENT
Those who are dead-set to win are likely to mark their cards.

A knave can win over a sage, if a fool is the referee.

[7]

The philosophical mind never wishes to win an argument, but rather the truth.

❦❦

Argument is a sure sign of conversation gone sour.

❦❦

Some argue to prove a point, others to prove themselves.

ARISTOCRACY

Leaning on ancestors proves most often that aristocracy hardly ever outlasts its first generations.

❦❦

A horse does not become a thoroughbred by chewing its oats without snorting, nor a man by genteel handling of knife and fork.

❦❦

What was good in aristocracies is long disappeared and what is left is good for nothing.

❦❦

There are no old families. Some got at the moneybag sooner, that's all.

❦❦

Those whose nobility is of their own making are the only true aristocrats.

ARROGANCE

Will create, in the strong, distaste; in the weaklings, admiration. What a weak era we live in!

❦❦

A racehorse strut ill becomes a donkey.

ART

Is man's feeble effort to imitate the Lord. Looking at certain canvases, I wonder if the Master is flattered.

❦❦

Dilettantes interpret art for art's sake as art for the artist's sake.

❦❦

Art for art's sake is like cake for cake's sake. It has to please someone or it is just a ragout of ingredients.

❧❧

Genius may be novel but novelties are not genius.

ASSOCIATION

Does not prove guilt but it indicates affinity.

ASTRONOMY

Is only the knowledge of the visible firmament. A new science is yet to come: the search for the worlds beyond our garland of galaxies.

ATHEISM

I hope for God's sake that He has not left Himself with man alone but has in other spheres better sons.

❧❧

God does not shun reason but evades the smart-aleck.

❧❧

To be of no God and rely on clever opinions is like having many acquaintances and no friend.

ATHEISTS

Are like the savage on an island who tells his family there is nothing beyond this rock but water and wind. One can live like that and die like that. But some of us have a hunch there is more to it than meets the eye and ear.

❧❧

Atheists brag that they can get along without God; this is hardly a distinction in an era where very, very few pay the Lord more than a Sunday call.

❧❧

Those who are not troubled by questions know all the answers.

❧❧

Atheists are often enough shamefaced antitheists. They wish no *Theos*, no God, no Principle to interfere with the petty advantages of their little existences.

Ⰷ

They can't find God because they search for Him only in the narrow confines of their traditions.

Ⰷ

The atheist steps on the hem of God and thinks he has stopped the heavens.

ATTITUDE
To a goat the most delicate garden is just a grazing place.

AUTHOR
It is imagination that makes a writer, not schooling, and you can't teach the first.

AUTHORITY
Must indeed rest on the majority, but on their reason, not their prejudice.

AUTHORSHIP
Too many speak who should be listening; too many write who should be reading.

AUTOBIOGRAPHY
May be history, if offered forthright; biography is mostly fiction, be it glib or ardent.

B

BABES

The Bible says you get the truth from them. Perhaps—if you get to them before they learn the ways of man.

BABY

When you first see it newborn it already has a life behind it of three-quarters of a year. It has suffered thirst and hunger, heat and cold, sour, bitter and sweet, tiredness, discomfort, indigestion and perhaps toxic illness. Sometimes it even completes its life span without ever setting foot into our world of rock and ether.

BEAUTY

Needs no explanation.

Beauty travels on many levels. There is a beauty seen by the heart, one seen by the mind, and one by the guts and sex glands. A steak can be beautiful and so can an architectural plan. I have even heard a physician exclaim: "What a beautiful eczema!"

BEGGARS

Are not the poor but the greedy.

BELIEF

Is measured by demonstration, not mere acceptance. Angels without wings are not in good faith.

BENEVOLENCE

Is the true ambrosia of the gods.

BIBLE

It is an odd book—the word of God, rituals of priests, legends, dull chronicles, and a sprinkling of childish lore—still, this poorly edited anthology has outlasted all the master epics. A book is just a bit of literature but the Bible is the very vessel of *Shekhinah*, the spirit of man, between heaven and earth.

It is an unfinished book. Who dares to say that Israel has yielded its last prophet?

❦❦

If the Book is not worth living by, it is not worth pretending by.

❦❦

Let God speak through the Book and bid the priests be silent.

❦❦

If the good Lord did not write the Bible, then King Solomon did, with some help from his father, David.

BIG MEN

Have the same problems as little ones, but on a greater scale.

BIOGRAPHIES

Are rarely worth reading. They are written by either flatterers or antagonists. At best they only give you the neighbors' opinion of the hero, or some imagined composite put together with clippings and transcripts. We often don't know what really motivates the soul of our nearest kin or acquaintance. Who dares to state with any degree of certainty what moved a man a century ago, a thousand miles away?

The biographer is like the man who longs to see the legendary lady in the castle window. She raises the blinds only when she is ready for you, all made up and dressed up and smiled up. From afar you can scarcely tell whether she is 17 or 70, and when you take a second look the blinds come down.

[12]

BLASPHEMY

It is not the blasphemer God minds so much as the "protector" of His honor.

BLESSING

I doubt if prayers can sway the Lord, but if love can move mountains it can touch the heavens.

BLIND

Love may be blind, but hate sees what is not there.

BODY CHEMISTRY

Its influence upon mental structure is sharply emphasized in the sudden change of attitude in man and woman right after the culmination of the sexual act.

BOOKS

Are like people: one man's revelation is to the other a meaningless bore.

Books are like people; it is not the number that matters, but the few that stand by.

Our libraries are getting bigger, which makes it more difficult to find a good book. The shelves are groaning under the pressure of clothbound nothingness.

A book is great by what you give to it, not take from it.

The truly great book does not find its readers, it creates them.

You may never find a friend, but you can always find a book. And with books as your friends, you will not go through life a lonely man.

Big books are like overgrown people—fine to stare at but little else.

⇜⇝

Books are the invisible tie between the people of the world. The Torah binds the Jews as the Koran the Moslems and the Gospels the Christian nations. Confucius bound the Chinese and so did Lao-tse and Buddha; until books were replaced by Marx's *Capital*.

The gods live in the books and where the books disappeared, the gods went with them. Gone are the Carthaginians, the Sumerians, and all their minor deities that never had a book of their own.

Books are all we have of the gods of the past, and of the present as well. And so the Book remains with us the ever-heritage of the tie with the heavens. Take away the books and you have a turmoil of people without unity or direction.

⇜⇝

Books are so long because the writers sell the harvest before they separate the wheat from the chaff.

⇜⇝

Perhaps the books of meaning should be bound in the scroll of antiquity to warn the reader they have been penned to touch the soul and not tickle the funnybone.

BORE

No man is boring who speaks of what troubles him.

BORROWING

The lender may lose a friend but the indifferent will never have one.

BRAINPOWER

Only a fraction of mankind's mental capacity is being used. The overwhelming bulk of the world's brainpower perishes unused because of totalitarian executions or war activities, because of a poverty-stunted literacy among seven-tenths of the population, and finally because of premature assignment to dulling labor. We are running the world on one cylinder instead of ten.

BRAVERY

Fear alone makes for bravery; the reckless show no virtue, only contempt.

BRIBERY

Let not the satiated judge the pressure of temptation suffered by the hungry.

BROTHERHOOD

Who is not his brother's keeper belongs not to the family of man.

❦❦

Be wary of the protagonist for brotherhood of mankind; likely as not, he pleads for love in terms of abstract billions of unknown foreigners because he never learned to love a small handful of his own people.

BUDDHISM

In its essence rests on four great principles, those of kindness, pity, communal joy and equanimity. Unlike Christendom, it managed to gain and retain loyal adherents without benefit of rack and faggot.

C

CABBALAH

The secret book of Hebrew tradition had no single author, nor had Torah nor Talmud. Its many authors wrote with sagacity which was not theirs but rather the reflection of the Divine Intellect they venerated.

❦❦

The Cabbalah teaches that in the realm of cognition and inner being there are ten different spheres. Not even all those who speak for truth see it on the same level.

CALMNESS

Let not the calm of indifference be mistaken for a mastered temper!

CANDOR

Some who wouldn't suffer a breeze delight in sending forth a tempest.

❦❦

Candor is insolence in a Sunday suit.

CAPITALISM

Has the rich and the poor; Communism, the poor and the poorer.

❦❦

I would rather take capitalism without a soul than Communism without a heart.

[16]

CARE
Who does not care has no care.

CATHEDRAL
The most imposing cathedrals are never too far from slums.

CAUSALITY
There are two causes of every effect; the visible one, and the real one.

CAUSE
It is a Cause that separates men from the mere mass.

CEREMONY
Is the outward sign of an inward duty. Some who deride ceremonials are merely covering up the tracks of their own egotism.

CHABAD
To understand the forces of the world is not enough. To gain access to the creative powers, the Cabbalah teaches, one must have wisdom and intuition (*chochma* and *bina*). Only the three combined—*chochma*, *bina*, *da-at* (*chabad*)—raise man above the material world.

CHANCE
Throws people together, man and woman, friend and foe. Chance makes kin and kings, a turned-up nose or a dusky skin, and places one's cradle in a mansion or a tent in the desert. From this unsorted mixture in the caldron of fate man draws his lot, his life and his luck. Yet some still like to think their dish was set out for them with deliberate intent by a providential hand.

CHANGE
Friends, work, leisure, convictions—man moves in a circle. Happy the man who can when need be jump his track for a wider orbit.

You may change man's conduct but not his conscience.

No man is the same for more than a fortnight.

CHARACTER

Is hard to determine, there are so many layers of pretense and prejudice hiding the core. Scratch the surface and you'll find the good are not so good, the bad not so bad.

Character gets no better with age, only more pronounced.

Character shows its color by our sins, not our virtues. The latter are too bland and lily-like.

Suffering may not make character, but kindness will.

Character must be seen in everyday life, not just in its Sunday best.

Tell me what you read and I'll tell you what you are.

It is when a man is in power that he shows his true direction and the measure of his patience.

CHARITY

Is not the effect of faith, it *is* faith.

Charity is the common denominator of all religions.

There is no charity so noble the cynic cannot impugn its motivation.

CHASTITY

Is honorable but charity is virtue come alive.

CHEERFULNESS

May be only a mood, but one for the better.

[18]

CHILDHOOD

The premature fruit may be much inferior to the slowly ripening.

CHILDREN

Perpetuate the prejudices and superstitions of their parents, rarely their wisdom.

❧❧

The newborn starts off with a score of notches on which to hang the good things in life. Watch the community load him with prejudice, malice and superstition.

❧❧

The wondrous adventures a child's mind can experience on a walk through a deserted, littered lot set between two old houses!

❧❧

Our ancestors called their newborn boy *Kaddish*, the Holy One. The child was their link to living eternity. Those who spend their existence without a child have no share in the fate of tomorrow's world. They circle around themselves with their backs to the future generations.

❧❧

To a child, its games of make-believe are as serious as our realities are to us. I sometimes wonder which of the two has more substance.

❧❧

There are no children, only young people.

CHOICE

At so many crossroads it's not a choice between good and bad, but between evil and greater evil.

CHOSEN PEOPLE

The pagans and gentiles begrudge the Jews their claim to a heritage which they themselves have been rejecting for thousands of years.

❧❧

The Jews chose God when no one else wanted Him.

❧❧❧

The Lord is not selective; the people are.

CHRIST

The greatest number of books have been written about one whom we know the least: Jesus Christ.

❧❧❧

One cannot be a Christian while living the life of a pagan. If your heart is pagan and your deeds are pagan, you remain outside the Circle of Christ, which means Church of Christ, no matter what prayers your lips speak, nor what the ikon before which you kneel.

❧❧❧

The Jews always have denied and forever will oppose the concept of God besides God. God is *Echod*, and One stands eternally for no more and no less, no picture of Him, no son of Him. This philosophy unendingly separates Judaism from Christianity.

❧❧❧

If He came to earth today, He would never forgive us, in all His celestial beatitude, for the unspeakable atrocities perpetrated on His kin and the kin of His mother and His faithful believers. All the paternosters and all the hymns of all fifty thousand saints and all fifty thousand theologians and all the genuflecting of a billion Christian knees, those alive today and those interred since the night of the catacombs, could not wear away the Jewish blood that is on Christian hands. If Jesus came to earth today, He would shrink from the Gothic cathedrals and the forest of church spires that carry the cross He took upon Himself that man might live a loving creature. Perhaps He would slink away to some little ghetto street in New York City, where there is a tiny ten-by-ten synagogue. And He would sit down with the other bearded Jews on the hard benches in this true house of worship. And He would read with the others from the ancient book of

Moses, which, as He said, He came to fulfill and not to destroy—the book of Moses, written in the script He could understand, written in the spirit in which He lived and for which He died.

☙❧

God lived with the world and its people for a million years before Jesus was born, so why begin time with the Son of God? Why not with God, the Father? There must have been good and evil before Christ came to earth; there must have been sin and repentance, devotion and derision, helpfulness and viciousness, manliness and gentleness and godliness; there must have been saints and thieves, Falstaffs and ascetics, foul men and sound men, naïve men and critics, the Lord's servants and the Devil's henchmen.

☙❧

There was a God before Jesus.

☙❧

Millions have died for Him, but only a few lived for Him.

☙❧

Jesus may have risen, but His followers stayed down.

☙❧

It is the same family in Little Rock that genuflects to Christ in front of the altar and to Satan in front of the schoolhouse.

☙❧

They suffer the cross He bore and go forth to impose His pains upon others.

☙❧

If His followers had been won by the point of a sentence instead of a sword, Europe's history were less sanguinary.

CHRISTIANS

Have failed for two thousand years to prove what Christ's teachings could do. From auto-da-fé to Auschwitz, a chain of *Miserabilia*. Nowhere else in history were such saintly words turned to such abuse.

[21]

CHURCHES
Are like umbrellas: a torn one is still better than none.

⋘⋙

Churches have lost the touch of the Divine and turned to book reviews and politics.

CITIES
Are like people: some are noisy and soon forgotten, others live on for a hundred generations after their homes and temples and streets are covered by silent sands.

CIVIL RIGHTS
Those who strain to hear a whisper from freedom infringed in our country seem to have a deaf ear for the screams of freedom outraged abroad.

⋘⋙

Civil rights do not include the privilege of undermining the inherent civility of democratic society.

⋘⋙

Civil rights are limited by civil duties.

CIVILIZATION
Can be judged by the value it places on human life.

⋘⋙

Civilization always seems to be at its peak to the present generation. I wonder what the ancients would say to our contemporary mass slaughters, torture and suppression.

CIVITAS DEI
The Lord will meet you halfway, but you must take the first step.

CLASSICS
The devotion to classicism is given to most great men. It is their deep-felt urge to strengthen themselves on the ancient eras of heroism, virtue and faith.

[22]

CLEANLINESS

Is a sign of respect for fellow man.

❦❦❦

Cleanliness is a consideration for others rather than oneself. For that reason, uncivilized people commonly are unclean.

CLERGYMAN

The preacher should be outstanding in Divine, not public, relations.

CLEVERNESS

Will set the mind ajar; wisdom will set it at rest.

❦❦❦

Cleverness is a poor substitute for understanding.

❦❦❦

Cleverness is competitive, wisdom never.

❦❦❦

Cleverness comes with the body, wisdom from the Lord.

COLOR

Man was made of clay. Clay is black or red, but never white. White man is a decadent creature, away from sun, wind and the sea.

COMFORT

Is the small benefit we derive for the most part from the deadly application of progress in science.

COMMUNISM

Welfare without liberty is only a plush form of enslavement.

❦❦❦

Communism is less a creed than an escape of the frustrated failure.

❦❦❦

Communism has driven off the captains of industry and replaced them with captains of demagogy.

❦❦❦

[23]

Communism began by incarcerating the few to free the many, and then enchained the many to protect the few.

≈≈≈

One of the great moral calamities perpetrated by the Communists is their having driven millions of persons to a flight into conformism, that is, phlegmatic acceptance of any and all directives coming from above without any wish for examination or criticism.

≈≈≈

Let's beware that in the struggle for the rights of man some not usurp the rights over man.

≈≈≈

Masterminds expropriated the state in the name of the people, and then expropriated the people in the name of the state.

COMPANIONSHIP

No one can afford to go to hell in his own fashion; Hades admits sinners in pairs only.

COMPARISON

Is the mother of envy.

≈≈≈

The great deeds are aroused by comparison. Free man endeavors to lead his life without comparison and thus without competition.

COMPASSION

Is the only one of the human emotions the Lord permitted Himself and it has carried the Divine flavor ever since.

≈≈≈

Those who do not feel injustice done to others are not part of the play the Lord has been ever staging. They are mere walk-ons in the scenes of history.

≈≈≈

It is a far cry from expressions of pity to acts of solidarity.

COMPETITION

This would be a more tolerable world to live in if men would merely go about their tasks instead of trying to be better than their fellow men.

COMPLIMENT

A trick coin carrying on its reverse the face of slander; a flip of circumstances, and there it is.

COMRADE

Watch out for the Utopian magician—he has an ax up his sleeve.

COMRADESHIP

What some refer to as unity is often but a bond of common hatreds and prejudices.

CONCEIT

The hill of progress is a baffling climb: at every turn, it seems, we have reached the top.

Conceit is the little man's substitute for self-satisfaction.

CONFESSION

Without repentance will institutionalize failings and pay sin a reward for pausing to consider.

Confession of an old sin neither improves nor elevates man; the task lies in facing honestly your present failings and egocentricities.

CONFIDENCE

Will reform more transgressors than punishment.

CONFORMISM

In the land of the one-legged, the two-legged is a cripple.

Conforming with even an only suspected evil is the opportunist's choice of the easy path instead of the right one.

CONQUEST

To conquer one's lust may sober the libidinous; to conquer one's hate is virtue itself.

CONSCIENCE

Human conscience is the only true moral guide, since all so-called ethical precepts, as well as religious commands, may be —and have been—turned as easily to evil as to good.

❧❧

Conscience is not a soft pillow to sleep on but rather a bed of pangs and restlessness. Only the indolent can sleep when evil prowls in the night.

CONSISTENCY

Is the program of dull minds.

CONSOLATION

At its deepest is silent.

CONSPIRACY

Ours is an age of conspiracy; no more is it the bulging prowess, the sharper blade, or the bluer strain of blood that claims a crown. It is the cunning tongue that sets a tyrant on the throne.

CONSTANCY

It is easier to be constant in hate than in love.

CONSTITUTION

A constitution is never better than those subscribing to it.

❧❧

Some of the worst tyrannies, such as those of Russia and China, have been built on the under-structure of an almost perfect constitution.

❧❧

A government is what it acts out, not what it pretends.

CONTENTMENT

Contentment is given only those who serve a cause.

❧❧❧

Contentment forever eludes the seeker of self-satisfaction.

CONTROVERSY

Frequently divulges little about the issues at stake, but much about the motives of those disagreeing.

CONVERSATION

Fixed ideas are the roadblock on the path of discussion.

❧❧❧

Conversation is only fruitful if all speak the same language.

❧❧❧

Those who make conversation destroy it.

❧❧❧

Conversation is sterile when motivated thinking dominates.

CONVERSION

The Jew who becomes a Christian or a Mohammedan or a Marxist because it admits him to a plush job in Vienna or Moscow, is like the rice-Christian in China—when the missionaries ran out of rice the Chinese ran out of Christianity.

❧❧❧

There is no need to drop Judaism for Christianity. Jesus never left the Jewish fold, but many times did the Christians desert Jesus. God lives in the faith of man, not in his churches.

❧❧❧

If you don't find God in your own faith, you will not find Him in a borrowed one.

CONVERTS

Torquemada and Hitler have made more converts of Jews to Christianity than all the missionaries of all times put together. Only dread and the rack could make them change the Star for a Cross and those who changed have not made Jewry poorer nor Christendom richer.

[27]

CONVICTIONS

Precious few are the masters of their convictions, great is the number of those mastered by them.

❦❦

He who says his convictions can never be shaken rarely stands on solid ground.

CORN

Truth is often corny; so is the staff of life.

COSMOGONY

They speak of the Origin of the Universe as if this tiny cosmos man sees were the Lord's sole domain.

God lives in infinite mansions man can neither see nor comprehend, and He is Being in essence, not to be fathomed or judged by animal creatures.

Man hunts and searches on his whirling globe and whenever he unearths a miniature truth within his environ, he thinks himself close to the peak of science. But this very pinnacle itself is only a speck of dust on the infinite plain of God's realm.

COSMOS

Physically, we are a swiftly deteriorating fungus settled on a dust particle whirling rhythmically in a black and empty barrel —I say "empty" because the distances between one tiny planet and the other are so gigantic that they are little different from stray, hardly visible dust-bits in an "empty" container.

And yet this fungus, riding for fleeting seconds on the dust of space, thinks his barrel a universe—nay, *the universe*.

COURAGE

If by some chance a true history of heroism were written, one would see a new array of faces that the world has kept in shadow: little men and women, from tents and huts and tiny flats, scrubwomen and peasants and clerks who suffered, sacrificed and gave their lives away for son or mother or friend. We have had a thousand histories of boisterous valiance, of herald, sword and crown—none yet of the humble carriers of the banner of courage.

❦❦❦

Courage is the conquest of fear, or else nothing but devil-may-care.

❦❦❦

Courage may sometimes be of doubtful issue, but cowardice never is.

❦❦❦

Courage ennobles man. This is not a world of aristocrats.

❦❦❦

It takes a few ribbons to make people die for their country. It takes much more to make them live for it.

COURTESY

May be a veneer, but neither is rudeness the real thing.

COURTIERS

Of old curveted about in the pageant of a monarch; today they strut in military tunics around the party boss.

COWARDS

May rise to heroism and heroes sink into oblivion, but dullards stay forever tepid.

CREATION

Is sudden evolvement—evolution is slow creation. The riddle of creative nature is still with us.

❦❦❦

Creation is so difficult to conceive and yet more so to deny.

❦❦❦

Some want us to believe the whole solar system grew out of an idly floating gas bubble. Still, whence the bubble?

❦❦❦

The earth could not have been more dismal and dank before creation, when God moved on the face of the waters, than it is

[29]

now. However, today through its formless bleakness runs a crimson thread.

❧❧❧

The worm in the stomach may have guessed from which glands the juices spring, perhaps also how they change and mingle and curdle. He may even reckon he knows the secret of creation.

CRIME

Deserves punishment; however, our punishment is but another crime.

❧❧❧

More crime is perpetrated within the law than without.

❧❧❧

There are no great criminals, only greatly misfortuned individuals. All crimes fit all people under altered circumstances.

❧❧❧

There is no crime so enormous that a better society could not have ameliorated it.

❧❧❧

They hunt the thief with a stolen rooster and name cities after plunderers of a nation.

CRITIC

A eunuch judging a man's lovemaking.

❧❧❧

A skydreaming eagle without wings.

❧❧❧

He lacks the courage to write; the critic's box is safe.

❧❧❧

A professional critic is like a professional mourner: his grievances are of dubious sincerity.

CRITICISM

Criticism is often furtive envy, veiled by dialectics.

CRITICS

Pygmies with poison darts live in the valley of the sleeping giants.

CRUELTY

Is not the beast in man, it is man in man. Animals know not cruelty, merely indifference.

❦❦

Cruelty is the coward's defense.

❦❦

Although they know hunger and fear, dumb animals know no cruelty; it takes training to make man evil, snide and cruel.

CURIOSITY

Is nothing more than appetite. It is the subject of which they partake that makes the difference between cannibals and people: some persons are curious to watch hangings, other persons are curious about ancient lands.

CURTAIN RAISERS

Four men who raised the curtain masking the heart of man: Solomon, Socrates, Shakespeare, Spinoza.

CUSTOMS

Are man's symbolic gestures to perpetuate his finest experiences in a world of fleeting time; the yearning for commemoration is the anguished urge to remain alive in the symbols of tradition.

CYNIC

Means "dog" in Greek; the Greeks had the word for it.

❦❦

A cynic is worse than a fool. The fool lacks insight but has faith; the cynic lacks both, though his cloak of impudence covers this emptiness.

❦❦

A cynic cannot see from here to tomorrow.

D

DANGER

Is an unpredictable guest: your loyal friend may be the inno-cent rock on which you stumble while your open enemy may cause your rise. Perhaps here lies the mystic meaning of "Love thine enemy."

DARKNESS

Is the cloth from which our little universe is spun. Away from the aura around this small globe, the spheres are bleak and cold. It is in us to reflect light and warmth; without us there is nothing.

DAY

A day is just a day, if even that. It is we who make it holi-, holy or hellish.

THE DEAD

Let not the dead bury their dead; they might rise again.

DEATH

Perhaps our fear of death is but embryonic fear of life.

⋙⋘

Death is a sideline guest who arrives and departs, but life comes to stay, with its thousand problems, difficulties and

obstacles. It is life that deserves our concern and ⟨
not death.

❦❦❦

Some persons make such great efforts preparing them.
for life, as if they were to go on living for a thousand y
They are so busy getting ready that they hardly get to liv.

❦❦❦

You have laughed God out of your schools, out of your
books, and out of your life, but you cannot laugh Him out of
your death.

❦❦❦

You still do your three score and ten, and then sink into dust
knowing not the why and wherefore of this fleeting dream-trot
in the arena of the human anthill.

❦❦❦

It matters less when we die than how much of our life will
live on.

❦❦❦

Man sometimes lives, but constantly dies.

❦❦❦

The thought of Life seldom occurs but at the time of death.

❦❦❦

From the day of birth we never stop dying.

❦❦❦

The fool dies only once.

❦❦❦

It is not the fear of death that saddens people, but the love
of life.

❦❦❦

While we dream we think we are being real; perhaps our
reality is only a kind of dream, and death the awakening.

❦❦❦

Death is a solemn reminder that life should be lived, not
spent.

❦❦❦

[33]

No man has nine lives but some die nine deaths.

⋐⋐⋑

Leave this world the way you found it: a heap of suffering and a drop of blessing. Don't run out without giving some of the latter—so many do.

⋐⋐⋑

Death is life's most persuasive reminder, and yet there are so many who can't read the message of the skull.

⋐⋐⋑

No man who understands death will misunderstand life.

⋐⋐⋑

There may be no life in death-time; there is certainly too much of death in life-time.

⋐⋐⋑

So many plot to become gravediggers of neighbor nations. The spade is patient; it will bury them all.

⋐⋐⋑

Death is too sudden a visitor in reality, but too rare a guest in our thoughts. Were he to visit man's mind more often, perhaps this would be a more somber but more gentle race.

⋐⋐⋑

Many a man whom life had treated shabbily, death raised to exalted heights—death, the silent arbiter over glory and oblivion.

⋐⋐⋑

Youth can experience death, but only age can experience dying.

DECEIT

Is like a rose; it smells sweetest when it is about to rot.

⋐⋐⋑

No one deceives us more often than we do ourselves.

DECISION

In most people is little more than awareness of which way the winds of desire blow.

DEEDS

Are God's measure of man, but people still use the Devil's currency of words, words, words, words. . . .

⟫⟪

One good deed may not beget another, but an evil deed will not beget a good one.

⟫⟪

If man is the image of God, then his deeds certainly belie His features.

⟫⟪

Deeds only matter in the final analysis. Some nations gave their all to build up the body, like the Spartans; others to develop the mind, like the Athenians. The Judeans, however, cultivated the God-bound deed, *Mitzwah*, the act humane.

⟫⟪

Better that your words follow you than run ahead of you.

DEFEAT

Can be fate's kindest admonition.

DELAY

In judgment is a victory for reason.

DEMAGOGUE

The sanctimonious voice of righteousness is standard with the demagogue. No sincere man has as honest a face as the professional confidence man.

⟫⟪

All tyrannical and demagogic undoings have their motivations. In fact in this motivation lies the root of the evil.

DEMIGODS

Judaism bars the crown of divinity from all and everything but the *Ruach Hakodesh*—the Holy Spirit—that is the One Eternal, the *Echod*. It places the crown upon the Torah, the knowledge of God, the indwelling of God in man; God alone is King.

[35]

DEMOCRACY

With corruption is better than tyranny without it.

⋘⋙

Democracy in its inherent toleration must be on guard against self-destruction.

DESIRE

Is given to all, discrimination to few.

⋘⋙

Desire is the appetite of the soul; it is not eating that makes for illness but poor diet.

⋘⋙

Desire alone can master desire. Ethics is a change of direction, not a change of nature.

DESPAIR

Is the mother of genius.

DESTINY

The vine dreams of climbing to the heavens—a twist in the wind and all is over.

⋘⋙

They speak of glory, but settle for notoriety.

⋘⋙

While they wait for it, the world runs away.

DEVIL

One may praise the Lord and serve the Devil.

⋘⋙

The worst thing about the Devil is that most people flatly deny his existence. Obviously he can thus do considerable damage to body and soul without ever being blamed.

⋘⋙

Devils must be running regular schools; there are so many people about of distinctly professional malevolence.

DIFFICULTIES

The Devil placed a thousand hurdles across the road to happiness, but man alone is still master of the mutual handicap.

DIGNITY

Takes a lifetime to acquire and a second to lose.

Dignity can be sold but not bought.

Dignity of the human person is the most meritorious aspect of democracy.

Dignity is a man-made respite of silence in a cacaphonic world of affront and fury.

Dignity of man is the tyrant's most serious obstacle—hence his appalling efforts to destroy it.

DIPLOMACY

Is the verbal technique of saying what you don't mean and making it mean what you don't say.

Diplomacy is a game of make-believe with malice aforethought.

DISAPPOINTMENT

Is a signpost to true values.

DISCONTENT

Has fired both holy vessels and unholy crackpots.

Discontent may become either spur or spite.

DISCRETION

Is the tact not to see what can't be helped.

DISCUSSION
Professionals here are as distasteful as in cards or sports.

DISEASE
Can be conquered but hate has to be dissuaded.

DISSENSION
Is disagreeable but it is hate that is the danger.

DOCILITY
Is one of the major social crimes cultivated in the average man and woman.

DOCTRINAIRES
Have more often offended the heavens with their deeds than unbelievers with their heresies.

DONOR
The greatest gift is the art of giving.

❧❧

Those who give quietly, give twice.

DOUBLE LIFE
We all lead it, only it is usually more multiple.

DOUBLE LOYALTY
Is often challenged by those who have none.

DOUBT
Is the space for thought to feed; but no mind can grow on space alone.

❧❧

Doubt is also a creed.

❧❧

It is amazing how some skeptics in one subject become gullible approaching another.

DREAMS

Some set themselves the task of putting dreams on the operating table; never were nightmares as lusty, reckless and fantastic as some peripatetic daydreams.

◈◈◈

Dreams may betray our instincts but daylight displays them.

◈◈◈

Dreams hide no secrets of which mind awake is unaware.

◈◈◈

What mysteries do the Philistines expect to find in their dream life if their real one is but commonplace?

DUELING

For a cause or trifle grew from the sport of men to the sport of nations.

DUTY

Duty is a virtue, but charity is the word of God.

E

EATING
Some fret about food as if salvation lay hidden in a vegetable.

ECONOMICS
Have hardly changed the people, but people have changed economy.

❦❦

Man, so imperfect in body and mind, demands perfection of all things in his social and economic structure.

ECONOMY
He who skimps on the seed will raise a poor harvest.

EDUCATION
Will eliminate foolishness but not deviltry.

❦❦

God has been separated from our schools; that may be all right, but the Devil was left there and that is not fair. The Devil of prejudice, arrogance, hatred, envy, home-grown superstition, and success-greed hovers over the school benches. You can't exorcise the Devil by looking the other way.

❦❦

Education in conscientious living will change the face of mankind; knowledge alone will only reshape the grimace.

❦❦

Perhaps one could teach goodness as one teaches algebra—or is there no logic to kindness?

❦❦

The thinking of people usually depends upon which side of their bread is buttered. This is especially true of the thinking done by the teaching profession in countries where the state administration does all the buttering.

❦❦

A man may be as smart as a book, and just as heartless.

❦❦

One need not be learned in the head to do the right thing, but rather learned in the heart. The learning of the heart is the most neglected branch of education today. The schools leave it to the churches and the churches leave it to the home, and how many homes are the proper place for character education?

❦❦

The heart can learn only from another heart. The printed word does not teach it.

❦❦

Education is in no way an indicator of moral responsibility; the intelligentsia of Germany avowedly supported Hitler, those of Russia supported Stalin and those of China support Mao, yet each of these dictators, by self-admission as well as irrefutable evidence, stands convicted as a mass murderer.

❦❦

The system provides for instruction in almost any field excepting human conduct. In some schools they even teach you how to use a camera and how to collect stamps, but how to live a free man's life is left to latchkey parents and the older gang around the block. They have bolted the front gate against God and religion, but the Devil sneaks in through the back door.

EGOCENTRICITY
Selflessness is the highest form of selfishness.

EGOTISM
The most difficult person to make friends with is yourself.

ELOQUENCE

Is these days a weapon, not a virtue.

EMANCIPATION

Of world womanhood is still to come. Ninety per cent of them are still bound by social and caste structure to lowly kitchen duty, which some day in the future will be taken over by automation.

EMPATHY

Those who say they feel for all, likely feel only for one, their very own one.

ENCYCLOPEDISTS

Cumulative erudition is more appropriate on a shelf than in a man.

ENEMIES

Are not those who hate us, but rather those whom we hate.

THE ENEMY

The character of mankind's foe changes from epoch to epoch. In earliest times anarchy was the great threat, the refusal of individual or tribe to respect the privileges of others. Pretentious usurpers were later the archfoes. Even religion for a while became a threat as suppressive organization. At present it is pretentious social welfare, sailing under the red flag of Communism, threatening to engulf mankind with a tyrannical net spread by cunning demagogues.

EPIGONES

Often appropriate the laurels that should adorn the originator.

EQUALITY

The Marxist system, on a platform of "no one with power over others," has created a spectacular One with power over all.

❧❧

Calling all citizens "comrades" may make some of them feel equal, but one glance from the boots of the peasant to those of the party leader will tell the difference.

≈≈≈

All men are not equal, but their rights are.

≈≈≈

All men are equal in sin, unequal in virtue.

≈≈≈

Equality before the law is often injustice before reality: to fine the rich the same amount as the poor works hardship on the poor, none on the affluent.

EQUANIMITY

Is sometimes a symptom of indifference and not of mastered emotions.

ERROR

The errors of today are still veiled; those of yesterday are an open book.

≈≈≈

Knowledge is frequently not truth but a lesser error.

≈≈≈

The great may go wrong, but they do not try to cover their tracks.

ETERNITY

It is beyond man's pale where time begins.

ETHEREAL

Even into the darkest soul passes, at least once in life, a ray of awareness of the supernatural, sometimes at the birth of a child or the death of a soul. Like to those living in ancient Egypt's *Amenti*, the land of the dead, through which passed once a day the sun god, Ra.

ETHICS

Man's study of nature will not improve his conduct; man's study of himself might.

❦❦

Physicists have improved the tempo of man but not his temper.

❦❦

If man would spend as much time on his soul as he does on his car, we would all fare better.

❦❦

People live on different wavelengths of time. Some live for the hour, others for the months or years, but few only for eternity. Long-range living is the way of true ethics.

❦❦

If you failed to learn ethics at six, you will not learn it at sixty.

EVIL

There is so much misery and massacre in this world that to deny it one is either a fool or a faker.

EVOLUTION

The protoplasm may be at the foot of evolution; man certainly is not its crown.

❦❦

We assume that only the fittest of each species survived, yet we find ourselves surrounded by multitudes of unfit creatures.

❦❦

Hate must be the highest form of emotion. We encounter so much of it now that we seem to stand on a peak of evolutionary progress.

❦❦

If man is the royal crown of creation, I am an anarchist.

❦❦

The neat classification of animal life into higher and lower forms is like the Social Register: it is all right with the people listed in it but hardly a proper guide for the Lord.

❧❧

The world has shifted in the last ten thousand years from an era of bestial primitives to one of highly educated beasts.

EXPERIENCE

If the dead were to rise and bury the living, I doubt if they'd make a better world. The only thing man seems to learn from experience is that it bears repetition. They killed the Czar to end tyranny, and began a free state with a new tyrant.

EYES

Can as well conceal a betrayal as betray what they conceal.

F

FACE

Man's countenance is the Lord's canvas.

FACTS

Are difficult to accept because they must be grasped; fancies are quickly taken on, since they require belief only.

FADDISTS

Use the reasoning of a scholar to prove a proposition little removed from old wives' fairy tales.

FAILURE

If you can do nothing with yourself, others are not likely to do better.

FAIRY TALES

The great tales were never written for the young. But our time has lost the spiritual naïveté of life, so only the children are left to respond to the significance of the ancient lore.

FAITH

There is no short cut to true faith; yet so many drop out into the easy byways of superstition and false beliefs.

❧❧

Faith will not waver where reason is its foundation.

❧❧

Faith fundamentally is given only to those who take the road of reason to the bitter end.

❦

Faith is nothing but knowledge that what we understand is only a shadow of the Unknown. Faith is the science of the pitiful limitations of man's mental scope.

❦

Faith has its weaknesses, but faithlessness is the poorest substitute.

❦

Adonai Echod! God is One, and the One lives in the heart of man, and the love to God and the love to man are one and the same. This is not only the beginning of true faith, this is all of it; the rest is silence.

❦

The man who has his own religion has a fool for a priest.

❦

Faith is belief in the invisible. It would be a dull world, indeed, if only the visible were reality.

❦

Faith and doubt are brothers under the skin.

❦

Faith is not proven by the number of believers. Abraham was alone and he had the truth against a whole generation of pagans.

❦

Faith must transcend the narrowness of a limited God given only to this, man's little world, and rise to adoration of *Elohim*, the God of Eternities, the Lord of infinite Universes.

FAME

Its seekers show that strange preference for notoriety among the many to appreciation by the few.

❦

The "No" of one expert outweighs the "Yes" of a thousand amateurs.

❦

Fame runs in circles. One can be burning with ambition within his little ring and be cold to the rest of the world.

❧❦

Fame spreads, elusive in the grasping arms of turbulent man until all the strength and time and breath inherent to mortals are spent in the embrace of the clothed chimera, and man is left nothing but a stumbling shadow of his true self.

❧❦

Fame cannot be possessed. It cannot even be arrested, and if some of the naïvely ambitious hold it for their own, let them take only one further look to find how precarious is their grip.

FAMILIARITY

Purity is not disturbed by a closer look; pretense is.

FAMILY

Relatives may become friends, but friends are always kin.

FANA-FIL-LAH

The Moslem saint's nirvana or annihilation in God is as little an ethical act as the ascetic seclusion of the Christian Trappist. An act exists as ethical or unethical only in relation to others. A flight into mystical hermitage may bring one peace or gratitude or forgetfulness but never is it a matter of morals. The saint is often more selfish than the sinner. Running away from the cares and battles of life may serve the interests of a burdened soul, but in the light of social morality it is just another deed strictly for the sake of the benefits it offers the doer.

FARM LIFE

Its idyllic aspects have been grossly overrated. The work of raising and tending kitchen requirements is hardly inspiring.

FASCISM

The path of the dictator is paved with democratic pronouncements.

[48]

FATALISM

The man who hates his enemies is no wiser than the child who hits at the chair over which he has stumbled.

FATE

Caesar thought that he cast the dice of fate, but to the far heavens in distant night it was merely one hill of ants robbing another.

❧❧

Fate holds this tiny globe in its giant palm, hardly taking note of the dust on it called man.

❧❧

The unpredictable fall of events in our erratic stream of life. Sometimes what looks like a whirling trap to certain doom throws us onto a most attractive shore and what appears a stretch of gentle caressing waves will drag the unsuspecting to perdition. You cannot tell what this goddess spins until the web is done and carried by the winds to the far-blue rocks of posterity.

FAULTS

It is not the faults we have, but those we see in others that make us intolerable.

FEAR

May be justified, but it will not bring justice.

❧❧

Who has the fear of God never had His love.

❧❧

Fear is the severest of pains, and the least alleviated.

❧❧

The unknown fears trouble us most.

❧❧

Fear means nursing a problem instead of facing it. It is a play of self-pity ignoring the inevitable. It takes courage to brush aside broodings of temerity. Our sages said that the courageous die by the blade, the timid by a thousand strokes of their fears.

❧❧

[49]

Those who endanger the safety of a state by their urge for power are prone to panic the people into fear of an imaginary enemy abroad.

❦❦❦

The face of the courageous is chalked with dread; it is only the reckless who know no anxiety.

❦❦❦

Some of the rich pay for having their minds diverted by analysts from fears to which the whole of the less affluent world is likewise subjected. The earth is full of fears beyond those pampered few; the task is not to shield the privileged, but to rise against all that is oppressive.

❦❦❦

Fears are not to be alleviated by hiring professional pacifiers, but eliminated by opposing the men or institutions that create them.

FEARLESSNESS

Is shown not so much by those who stoically accept an inevitable verdict of death, but rather by those who could escape the death penalty if they would only submit.

FEELING

Perhaps the Cabbalist was right when he said: Feelings slumber in the throat; the weighty ones sink to the heart and the light ones fly out through the tongue.

FELLOWSHIP

You are what you arouse in fellow man.

FELLOW-TRAVELERS

They are so eager for perfection in social order that they accept chaos as a substitute provided it holds forth a promise for tomorrow.

FLAG

The American flag is a symbol, not of the nation, but of its freedom.

FLATTERY

Flattery is the first step on the road to slander.

❧❧❧

Flattery is like an ill wind; it shifts without pause.

❧❧❧

Men who tolerate flattery will never accept criticism.

❧❧❧

Flattery is a scheme of the sly to bribe real people with make-believe currency.

❧❧❧

The tongue that flatters is the tongue that poisons.

FLIGHT

Man still has failed to gain the secrets of muscle-powered bird flight although he has mastered the winds; just as he has conquered the waters by use of the boat, but not learned to swim like the fish.

FLOWERS

Petals that light up a feeling of beauty in one nation are just feed in another.

FOE

There is no better friend than a frank enemy.

FOLLY

One man's folly is the other man's faith.

FOOLS

Are not those who know little but rather those who know too much of what just isn't so.

❧❧❧

Men are fools, but not so much as those who think themselves exceptions to this dictum.

[51]

FORCE
Has made slaves of men but it is courage that makes men of slaves.

FOREIGN LANGUAGE
It's knowing a people's troubles and hopes that brings one close to them, not the speaking of their tongue.

≈≈

With the number of platitudes and irrelevancies being spouted by mouth and pen in any one language, the acquisition of additional tongues should be soundly discouraged.

FORESIGHT
Improve your hindsight and you will gain in foresight.

FORGETTING
The art of forgetting is as important as that of remembering.

FORGIVENESS
Is an act of grace to the aggrieved, not the aggressor.

≈≈

The infant and the dying show the look of forgiveness— Eternity smiling at man's pitiful self-importance in coming and going.

≈≈

Forgiveness is a decision no longer to see the evil; forgetfulness is understanding it as a part of the chain of woe.

≈≈

Can you forgive the snake its poisonous fangs, the tarantula its sting, the leopard its claws? Such is man to man.

≈≈

If it's divine to forgive, it's manly to forget.

FORTUNE
Has no rhyme or reason, like the rock that falls on an ant-hill. Perhaps the surviving ants think they were saved by divine providence and send up hymns of thanks.

≈≈

Fortune, more than rarely, is great misfortune.

FREE MEN

Are bound by a thousand chains of conscience, love and duty; it is the slave to himself who stumbles through life unattached and careless, given to loose talk and loose thinking.

FREEDOM

Is the sole touchstone of social progress: a Communism that requires enslavement in order to gain freedom is like virtue predicated on crime.

❦❦

Free men have no right to live and work in isolation if they wish to retain the bliss of their heritage. Rather is it their duty to crash into the lairs of the slave-makers and slave-holders, so that the rest of the world may become free and stay free.

❦❦

Freedom lies not in the resignation to want, but rather in the accession to true values.

❦❦

Freedom is not dominant where subjugation still exists, even in a corner.

❦❦

Freedom knows only pro and contra with no neutrality in between.

FRIEND

Wheat does not come without chaff. If you want your friend, accept his entourage.

❦❦

One friend is worth a thousand acquaintances.

FRIENDSHIP

Too often are close relationships founded on dislike and envy called friendships, for we are bound to those we hate almost as much as to those we love. Perhaps hatred is an even stronger tie than affection; it is more lasting, and like love, seeks out its object, yearning to dwell in its shadow.

❦❦

Like the Stone of Wisdom, friendship may be lying right in your backyard and you may never know it.

❦

Those who cannot give friendship will rarely receive it and never hold it.

❦

Your friend is the one who sees you as you would love to see yourself.

❦

Friendship is a daydream beat of the heart for a face that lights it up. Only in dreams can one see in that simple trifle all virtues, valiance and varied attributes that warm the clasp of the hands. In the light of friendship, the commonplace fades into a serene glow and banality metamorphoses a romance. What touching reality in such dreams, and how barren existence in mere objective togetherness!

❦

Meet with your friends in the core of the matter, where you agree, and not on the fringe where you differ.

❦

Man's greatest gift to man is man.

FUTURE

For a better tomorrow you have to better today.

❦

The best way to look ahead is by looking back.

❦

If you understand your past, the future will hold no riddles.

G

GAB

Some gabble with the tongue, others with the pen.

⋘⋙

Every sinner was punished by the good Lord with a handicap: the dullard got the gift of gab.

GAMBLING

A gulp from the bitter brew of fear and hope to give some taste to a dull existence.

GENEROSITY

To find fault in our heart is easy; to find generosity in it is difficult.

⋘⋙

Generosity in the hands of the cunning is a weapon, not a virtue.

GENIUS

True genius is a servant of his cause, not its exploiter.

⋘⋙

Genius is no part of madness, but madmen may have genius.

GIFTS

He who gives too much belittles the recipient.

[55]

GLORY

Who pants after fame will sooner or later run out of breath.

❧❧

The sweet smell of military victory has, like all perfumes, a very putrid matter as base.

❧❧

The difference between gangsterism and imperialism is mainly in scale. The attacks of Hitler on Poland or Stalin on Finland, Alexander's plundering of Asia, Titus' sacking of Jerusalem or the banditry of the Vandals, the Vikings, the Normans, the Huns, the privateers of Queen Elizabeth, etc., etc.—it is only the size of these sanguinary excursions and the loot that distinguishes them from common holdups. Take off their gilded armor, fancy tunics, pretentious crowns and ludicrous rationalizations and before you stands a motley lot of bandits with tribal support.

Undraped of the purple, and marshal's shako, what we commonly teach and tell as history is only a series of criminal cases in which the victim is lampooned and the gunman glorified.

True history is yet to be written.

GOD

Is not worried about His enemies, I feel, but some of His defenders are frightening to behold.

❧❧

There is no need to cling to God every moment of the day, but never to veer too far away from Him—that is steady virtue.

❧❧

The essence of all Being is One, and there our wisdom ends. But this we feel and know as well as we, with our little souls, can grasp the thought: the way to God is man's love to man.

❧❧

The soul of God is in the soul of man. There is no God but in the consciousness of innermost man.

❧❧

God has no interpreters but man's hearkening, and the church may or may not speak His voice. The voice of God is too high for some to hear and too low for others, and it does not exist at all for the many, many who are deaf. The voice of God may speak through the morning green of a sun-kissed meadow, the melancholy rhymes of bittersweet poetry, the angry shouts of a dying soldier giving his life on the battlefield altar of freedom, the years of parental drudgery and filial sacrifice, heavenly sermons and songs leaving the lips of the truly inspired, the words of wisdom of sages then and now.

There is no God besides the God in the depths of man's mind. There is no love and inner freedom but that which springs from the fountain of truly divine cognition. There is no unity but the everlasting truth borne by man's inner self.

Man lived without God for a million years. He now dwells in the presence of God, but does God dwell in the heart of man?

The ancient Hebrews did not write the name of God. I often wish the Christians would follow suit, as never was a word more misused in writing and speaking than the name of the Lord.

If modern man understands the Ways of the Lord, then the Master is in a bad way.

The small mind envisions a smallish God and then denies Him. One has to be a big man to see God in His glory, a very big man indeed.

The Hebrews have no name for Him, the Moslems have a hundred. Both suggest the same thing, that there are concepts as well as emotions that can be communicated only allegorically.

[57]

God is poor company for those who don't speak His language.

❦❦

God moves in deepest silence over the sands, the oceans and the sod. Only the thirsty soul will spy His footprints.

❦❦

God is a silent partner in this world, and man certainly gives Him the short end.

GODHEAD

To get nearer to God, come closer to man.

GOLDEN MEAN

Those who follow the golden middle way often have a profound appreciation of the value of gold.

GOLDEN RULE

Do unto others as you say you do.

GOOD CHEER

Is not virtue but a step toward it. Baal Shem-Tov, the Hebrew mystic, said: "I can sing a prayer as well as say it."

GOOD TIMES

Some people bear up worse under good times than under bad.

GOODNESS

Is held in such low regard it takes courage to profess it.

GOSSIP

We need not know a man's personal follies to understand his philosophy.

GOVERNMENT

By observation is the so-called People's Democracy. The citizens are apprised of various governmental changes or edicts;

[58]

they don't have any part in making them, they are merely observers!

❧❧

Tyrants have often ruled in the name of the people; democracy, however, is based on the people ruling themselves.

❧❧

Government where there is no opposition cannot be a people's government.

GRADING

That we have great men in our time and recent times is not because of our educational system, but rather in spite of it. They are the ones the teachers couldn't spoil. At least they couldn't spoil them altogether, although some important figures of our times bear the mark of moral confusion and anti-social behavior. Some of them use their gifts and talents to sing the praise of totalitarian dictators. Others do not hesitate to undermine and betray the welfare of the democratic community they live in.

How can it be otherwise in a society in which the teachers have not yet learned that youth raised in ambition, self-assertion and competitive avarice will not grow into charitable adulthood. And if some think that they can beat more knowledge into youth by the scourge of the contest than by mere teaching, I would say that an ounce of human kindness is worth a ton of so-called knowledge. It isn't that you need the scourge to train the youth, just as it isn't the whip you need to keep man at work. Give man a proper job and a proper wage and freedom to live in, and he will stay at a task until it is done, because man is made to work. And give a child answers to his curious mind in open manner and in proper time, and give him freedom to query and freedom to participate in equal manner with all his classmates without fear of being degraded, without bribe of rank promises, and the child will follow your teaching eagerly, because youth wants to learn.

Does a father grade his children? Does he mark them low and high, passing and failing? They are his to teach and love

[59]

alike. And if teachers lack the color of speech or the power of persuasion to entertain the interests of the young, perhaps they should seek for other fields of work instead of holding school over a herd of uneasy scholars, and leave teaching to those who feel the calling and have the cordiality of the teaching mind.

GRAMMAR
The best grammarian still can't write a verse.

❦❦

Grammarians make no new thoughts, but thoughts make new grammar.

GRANDPARENTS
Are the lost branch of this generation; the offspring does not rightly know where to place them on the family tree.

GRATITUDE
Such is the soil of man's heart that you may plant the sweetest seed and harvest stone.

❦❦

People who set out to hurt you will, in the long run, help you as often as those who desire to be of assistance may harm you.

❦❦

Gratitude forever faces the obstacle of envy.

GRAVE
The real hero dies a silent death and lies in an unmarked grave.

❦❦

If the epitaphs were but half true, this were the best of worlds.

GREAT IDEAS
Were never discovered by one man, but often halted by one.

GREAT THOUGHTS
Ever walk the open road. Pretenses seek out the misty byways.

[60]

GREATNESS

There are great stages in a little man's life and small moments in the life of the great.

Big people are sometimes small men and little people are often really big.

Greatness lies less in the skill to succeed than in the ability to accede.

Raising yourself is a skill, raising your fellow man is a virtue.

Great men are simple, but what intricate simplicity!

GRIEF

Can only be cured by reason, and reason rests with God.

Those who do not care easily master their grief.

To suffer grief may be unavoidable; to inflict it is not.

GUILT

The feeling of guilt is the gateway to virtue.

Man is equal to any crime or sin under given circumstances. Those whom fate spared or favored are inclined to condemn in haste the one who drew a bad lot.

Guilt by association is not conclusive, but considerable. I think little of the virgin who spends her days in a brothel.

Some of the most unspeakable crimes leave telling marks but no telling evidence.

Lack of punishment is no proof of innocence.

H

HACHUKKIM

Some of the laws of the Torah cannot be rationally justified. Perhaps some of them had only one purpose, to make all the people of the country do the same thing at the same time with the same devotion—a practice in discipline and religion, a training in unity and obedience to higher principles.

HANDS

Beware of the grip that is too firm; it may be calculated.

HAPPINESS

Is no criterion for either health or wisdom; the foul and the fool can be happy as a drunken sow.

Happiness to be true must be oriented on landmarks much greater than one's own little personal joys and gratifications.

Perhaps hogs are happy, but man should be moved by a greater wish than to be jolly.

Happiness is not a virtue, but virtue brings happiness.

Happiness is determined by the number of people one loves.

Happiness is a task, not a gift.

⤞⤝

The rich are no happier than the poor—only more comfortable.

HASTE

Those who run through life will get there quickly, but hardly well-composed.

HATE

Dictators long ago found out it is easier to unite people in common hatred than in common love.

⤞⤝

Hate binds no less than love. The free man will want to put it behind him. Hatred disfigures your lips no less than your words.

⤞⤝

One who hates an evildoer fails to recognize that those with ill will, more often than not, serve us instead of their own interests.

⤞⤝

One may avoid, confine or punish a culprit without snarling. To love an enemy, however, is absurd; it is difficult enough to love one's friends.

⤞⤝

Whatever you love, you are its master; whatever you hate, you are its slave.

⤞⤝

Hate ignores the wise truth that all evildoers are such by necessity. They do need to be curbed, like thorns or thistles, but in weeding hate is unwarranted.

HEART

Is the mind's bridge to wisdom.

⤞⤝

The world is full of ailing hearts; quacks abound and rare is the doctor.

[63]

HEAVEN

The Cabbalah speaks of ten steps to heaven. There is modesty, and courage, and devotion, and so on. The book never mentions libido as a rung to beatitude.

THE HEAVENS

Are not the seat of God but a reminder of His unseen Presence.

HELL

Cannot outdo mankind's own mutual bestiality.

HELP

The man who needs no one's help is a lonely man indeed.

Helping one has to learn, even as one has to learn how to harm; it is only indifference that comes to man naturally.

HERITAGE

You can tell a thousand years later when a great man left his imprint on the mind of a nation.

HERMIT

The hermit is a dull man preoccupied with nothing but his little self, be it physical, be it spiritual. The wise man, like Socrates, seeks out the people of the world and makes them part of his own self, the greater Self of the greater man.

HERO WORSHIP

Has an uncanny tendency to choose scoundrels as the object of adulation.

HEROES

Don't rise, they are raised.

True honor does not crave recognition, as true wisdom

craves not publicity. The great heroes and the great men of wisdom walk silently through the bypaths of mankind.

※※

Some of those buried in prison yards deserved mausoleums, and many of those entombed in cathedral sepulchers should have been thrown to the jackals. The tombstone tells when you died, not how you lived.

HEROISM

The hero is not a man without fear, but one who hates injustice more than he loves personal safety.

※※

The man who will risk his life on a childish dare may not do the same if the welfare of a whole nation hangs on it.

HISTORY

Half the world is still engaged in the ancient struggle for freedom from the shackles put on by usurping ideologues. The wrathful gods of old stepped aside for Karl Marx, but the Red princelings differ little from the celestial ones in applying scorpions and the lash to the lowly.

※※

Frequently in history the burden rested on men behind the screen; the fancy and proud actors on the stage were only marionettes.

※※

History of our global events is merely an insignificant whisper on the fringe of the titanic battles of the cosmos, our blood-and tear-soaked earth but a splinter falling in the aeonic conflicts.

※※

History repeats its mistakes but not its accomplishments.

※※

Of the lives of the oppressors in history there should be only one brief note identifying their tenebrous existence; the rest of it, with castle, equestrian statue, fancy dress with crown and mace and bloody sword, ought to go into a black book filled with

[65]

horror tales and pitiful songs. Social understanding lies in searching for the life and work and suffering of the little people whose memory seems all but buried beneath the showy tinsel of the people's malefactors.

❧❧

There are too few books from the pen of those who made history and too many by those who poorly retraced it.

❧❧

Every historian writes as if his little country were the center of the globe—and nothing can convince him otherwise.

❧❧

History should be taught backwards. It makes for a more somber panorama. We did not climb from rags to riches. We still fight for waterways and island rights like growling cavemen, we grovel before arrogant overlords and sneer and hiss at men of other color.

❧❧

History is a planless sequence of little events and situations. Had England remained a peninsula, as it was not so long ago, Napoleon might have conquered all of Europe and the British Empire perhaps would never have come to be.

If the Czar had executed Lenin instead of imprisoning him, Russia likely would have stayed a liberal socialist country under Kerenski.

If the Babylonian Jews had come to the rescue of beleaguered Jerusalem in the year 70 instead of defaulting on their promise of assistance, Judea would perhaps have lived on, and its people would not have been dispersed. Vespasian had no more Roman armies to spare.

A thousand little things—a poorly directed dagger or bullet, a geographical oddity, a quirk of circumstance—and the world would have taken a different shape.

❧❧

History has three sides to it: the wrong side, the right side, and the way it really happened.

❧❧

Glory is the most precious gift posterity can bestow upon its deserving ancestors. It is one measure which even the most powerful of potentates can neither falsify nor escape. If there is any glory to the Imperium Romanum, it lies in the ruins of the temples which they destroyed, not in the gory epics of their conquests and victories. I do not wish to know the ugly details of how the mercenary legions vanquished neighbor after neighbor. I do not want to know the sinister data of their evil hierarchy that began with Romulus and ran its sanguinary course through the Western world for a thousand years and more. I say it matters little what Caesar befouled his own mother and what Messalina put womanhood to shame. Furthermore, I would say that all that type of history is not a history of the people, but rather of its exploiters, its usurpers, its false prophets.

The wars of conquest by self-appointed or family-perpetuated masters over an enslaved people are not the history of the world, but rather the story of man's iniquity and unspeakable cruelty to fellow man. The hardships and tortures with which usurpers and their ilk terrorized mankind are a terrible, but only a single, chapter in the great book of the story of man, to be read like the verse on Purgatory as a reminder and a lesson. The story of man begins where the chapter of tyranny ends and he who embellishes the misdeeds of the blackguards, be they ancient or of recent vintage, teaches not history but the perversion of it.

Come forth, the man to tell the story of the little people, people that till the earth and raise the fruit, that fish in the ocean and lakes and rivers and hunt in the forests and breed the stock and trade in the markets and make a thousand things of use or of pleasure for man and child. Come forth, the man to tell the story of these people, the real people, those that work and those that pray, those that wander and sing and play and lead the good life and have fellowship in their hearts and sincerity in their hands.

These are the people who deserve the glory that posterity can bestow. Their world should be written about. How they fared and how they failed should be related in the books of history, and not, certainly not, all that plush and plunder, that weird twosome of tournament and dungeon that signifies the era of courtly tyranny blighting mankind like the plague it was.

❦❦

There are as many versions of history as there are nations, and then some.

HOBBY
Is a man's endeavor to make an avocation give him the satisfaction an occupation should.

HOME
The home one runs away from is none.

❦❦

Home is where your friends are.

HOMILETICS
I wish they would remember that Moses was a poor speaker; still his was the voice of God.

HONESTY
Toward oneself is rare indeed.

❦❦

The confidence man has honesty always on his lips.

HONOR
Is so frequently bestowed upon the wrong, the false and the scheming that it has become a prize rather than a virtue.

❦❦

Honor and dignity are matters of cognition, not recognition.

HOPE
Is the attractive escape-hatch from the harsh alternative to do or die into a world of tranquilizing daydreams.

❦❦

Fear is the mother of hope.

❦❦

Whatever betterment we have today was carved out of a world of stone by men of the hammer, not men of hope.

❦❦

Hope may ease the troubled conscience but not the trouble itself.

❦❦

Where faith takes no decisive action, decision is left to fate.

HOSPITALITY

Remember, the man with whom you converse is a guest at your mind.

HOSTILITY

Begins at home. If school does not eradicate it, life has little chance.

HUMBLENESS

Before a principle is the measure of a man's faith and character.

HUMILITY

It takes a lot of thought to fathom human knowledge, and rare intellectual humility to realize that the greatest depth of man's thinking still runs only in shallow grooves.

HUMOR

Is a gracious arbiter.

❦❦

Humor is the harbinger of persuasion; lack of it foretells discord.

❦❦

A sense of humor is sense for sure.

❦❦

Humor is the daughter of reason; she makes game of self-important pretentiousness.

HUNGER

Surveying the last four decades, one would say that the Communists are more adept at putting lead into bodies than bread.

❦❦

Hunger is the father of servility.

HYPOCRISY

Where terror reigns, hypocrisy will raise its changing faces.

I

IDEA

The world may be only an idea of mine, but my idea is not this kind of world.

IDEALISM

Idealism is an approach to life, not an end to itself. One can be quite materialistic about so-called ideal things, such as religion, literature and the arts. On the other hand, one can be quite idealistic about material things, such as the living conditions of the working or farming man.

IDEAS

Are a versatile metal that can be beaten into plows or swords, or hammer and sickle.

Words, profound and meaningless, pop out when thought fails.

More people have died for false idols than true ideas.

IDENTITY

Basically, all people are alike. That is perhaps the cause of their constant squabbles and feuds; they dislike in each other their own debilities.

IDLENESS

Don't kill time—you may yet discover you could have used it.

❦❦❦

Idleness is preoccupation with the barnacles of thought.

IDOLS

If it be true that one becomes like what he worships, what monsters this world's idols must be!

IGNORANCE

It is not the ignorant who forever keep the Devil's brew boiling, but rather the wiseacres and their erudite friends.

❦❦❦

Most people don't care enough to search for the facts of the issues they talk about with such concern.

ILLUSION

If this be all just an illusion, take away the world and leave me my dreams!

IMAGINATION

Reality—what a poor substitute for imagination!

❦❦❦

Imagination is the arena of the genius.

❦❦❦

Science, too, must ride Pegasus—diligence its legs, but imagination its wings.

❦❦❦

Heaven is a matter of imagination but so are hate, love, and pretty much everything else.

IMITATION

Is nine-tenths of our cultural pattern.

IMMORALITY

Acts of animalism are nothing more than that; immoral they are not. Immorality occurs only when there exists an antagonistic tendency or act against society.

IMMORTALITY

Is no more fabulous than birth: that out of dust and dirt can rise an organism of a billion muscles, nerves and bones, to talk and walk and think and then dry up and bury itself back into a hole of dirt and dust. Who can fathom the whereto and wherefore of life immortal?

In passing away we only take to the heavens what we leave to mankind.

The truly great from Lao-tse to Spinoza never discussed life after death, only before it.

IMMUTABILITY

Great men die but great ideas live on.

INDEPENDENCE

Is the wish of a peasant: to raise porridge with his own two hands.

The free man wants to live, create and work in interdependence. Man is to man a Devil but sometimes a God.

INDIFFERENCE

Being wrong is no disgrace, being indifferent is.

There is no greater temptation than that of indifference.

INDOLENCE

Takes others for granted, but graver yet is the consequence of taking oneself for granted.

AN INFIDEL
Is one who does not accept the superstitions of his community.

INFLUENCE
There comes a time when the twig can no longer be bent.

INHIBITIONS
If we could *see* desires, if greeds and lusts, hates and envies, jealousies and revulsions, the whole array of human feelings had a corporeal form, this would be an impossible world; it is the sobering social inhibitions that make coexistence tolerable.

❦

It isn't the lack of inhibitions that distinguishes man from man but rather the choice of inhibitions. The lack of inhibitions merely distinguishes animal from man.

INSANITY
It has become downright modish to claim a touch of madness. Some women speak of their psychiatrist as of their hairdresser or modiste—a sort of confessor-in-waiting.

❦

Insanity is a frequent visitor of genius under stress, a strange guest of the lonely in their flight from reality.

❦

The insane mind has as many variations as the sane; sometimes I wonder which one contributes more to the madness of the world.

❦

For the very same actions and expressions some were declared to be suffering from religious mania, others were called saints and divines.

INSTRUCTIONS
Teach kindness and you reap intelligence; teach hate and you reap prejudice.

INTEGRITY

They teach you early how to wash your face and body, in school and home, but how to cleanse your mind of putrid ideas and prejudice, that is left unsaid and thus undone. I am afraid that even the occasional ablutions in the church are scarcely purifying, no more than face-saving. They walk about with shining faces and decaying souls.

INTEMPERANCE

Is an annoyance, but controlled enmity is something to look out for.

INTERESTING

Even the dullest is interesting when speaking his mind honestly; it is the scintillating surface conversationalist who is the intolerable bore.

INTUITION

Is thinking ahead, as reason is thinking back.

ISSUES

Handle people with gloves; but issues, bare-fisted.

J

JAILS

Stables designed to improve ethics by herding together the sinners. As sin will always come out on top, the result of this process is invariably the acquisition of at least one new sin by the old sinners.

⟞⟞

You cannot make a man straight by cuffing him to crooks.

JEST

Is but honeyed criticism.

JESTERS

Are of two different brands: those with wit and those with venom.

JEW

What blasphemy is the theology of crucifixion—to paint the Jew as the destroyer of religion when the Jew is really its creator!

⟞⟞

Jews have been stunted in their growth by a hostile world from the days of Israel, the God fighter. They were chosen by the Lord to carry the Tablets of the Law, but their neighbors wanted them to carry the cross, or the banner of the crescent.

The chosen ones were decimated, decade after decade, century after century, with forced conversion, rack and pyre and noxious gases, and what could have been by now a nation of a hundred million children of Israel, is left a poor tenth after two millennia without grace and charity.

~~~

Many attribute to the Jews their own failing and then hate them for it.

~~~

Jews are the heart-people of our era. Could you see Jesus as a German, Frenchman or Chinese? Or Paul as a Japanese or Scotsman?

~~~

Everybody meets the kind of Jew he expects.

JEW-HATRED
You can't be a Christian and an anti-Semite, because Jesus was a Semite before he declared himself Christ.

JOURNALISM
Is characterized no less by its topics than by their treatment.

JUDAISM
Has no sects, only attitudes. What does it matter where one meets God and His Beatitude, be it in one great principle or in numerous precepts and legends?

~~~

Judaism is the story of a great father popularized by two difficult offspring.

JUDGMENT
Listening to both sides does not necessarily bring about a correct judgment.

JUDGMENT DAY
If only the Earth could heave off her coat of green and show the billion wounds of her interred children which men have inflicted.

~~~

[77]

To resurrect the nations underground would be as futile as making the living stay on forever. Let tomorrow's youth be raised on deeds of kindness, and the rest forgotten.

JURY
An untrained group of balance-keepers upholding the truth hidden by shady lawyers.

JUSTICE
Is the handmaiden of government and thus bespeaks the character of its master: the vilest tortures have as often been declared law as the loftiest precepts.

*

In certain countries, judges seem to act according to predicament, not precedent.

*

Justice is more a question of attitude than fact.

*

Stand on the side of the weaker and you'll always be on the right side.

*

Justice is a poor substitute for compassion.

*

Justice is like a greased pig: many touch it, few hold on to it.

JUVENILES
Will drift into delinquency if there are no chores to do, no tasks cut out. America has eliminated the apprentice shop for the nonstudious. The towns are full of idle juveniles who are kept *per forma* in school but *realiter* in the gutter. The truant at thirteen might better be an apprentice at fourteen than a delinquent schoolboy.

K

KEENNESS
It takes a rough stone to sharpen the edge.

KERA
They all have it, *Kera*. The Cabbalists refer to it as one eye on the realms of glittering everyday values. Few are the star-eyed with only one Lord, one aim and one love.

KINSHIP
A man after my own heart means a man with my own prejudices.

KLAN
Jesus never stopped in Georgia but Lucifer did.

KNOWLEDGE
It takes a lot of knowledge to understand how little we know.

❧❧

Learn what you know and not what is alien. Can the worm in the stomach see the light of the moon?

We think in the light of our planetary group of rocks, which we euphemistically call "the universe." This is as little the Universe as man's stomach, although the latter may appear as the world of worlds to a worm or germ.

All conjectures beyond our firmaments of space and thought

are theological dream-spinning and no more, fantasies of one fungus on a speck of dust talking to another on the nature of powers beyond.

❦❦

There is no knowledge—only a lesser state of ignorance.

❦❦

Knowledge *may* be good; kindness is good.

❦❦

Knowledge dwells in three mansions: the house of words, the home of facts, and the niche of wisdom. It is the last only that harbors peace of mind.

❦❦

Only the ignorant know everything.

❦❦

Some are satisfied when they hear it, some when they see it, and others stop when they have a Greek word for it; only too few go beyond the word.

[80]

L

LABOR

The many live for it so the few may live off it.

The laborer is not a better man than the capitalist, only less fortunate.

Tyranny of labor is no better than tyranny of military or industry.

LANGUAGE

Barriers are not what separates mankind: so many who speak the same tongue don't speak the same language.

You may use the same words and still speak a different language.

The Yugoslavs understand Russian and the Russians understand Yugoslav, but neither understand the other.

Language makes not the man; it is the man who makes language. Perhaps our schools would do better to guide the young in a search for the truer thought, the deeper concept, instead of a better syntax.

LAST WORDS

May your last words be like your first: a cry for the nearness of loved ones.

LAUGHTER

Brings tears into your eyes. It is the twin sister of weeping; oftentimes they are so close together, you wonder which way to turn.

LAW

Is as varied as the sentiments of those who rule.

A law is as proper as the motives of the ruler.

The law is never holy but often sinful. And perhaps even today, in this freest of countries of all times and places, there may be many who stand on the wrong side of the law, placed thus not because they went astray, but rather because the law strayed from the right path.

It is the lawbreakers in our history who have brought to the people of the Western world the rights they enjoy, and if the enchained East is to come to its freedom, it will again be the lawbreakers who will tumble the overbearing colossus of legitimate totalitarianism.

The law is the crime it purports to prevent.

It is with the breaking of the law that the freedom of man began; the bills of rights were written with the blood of heretics and lawbreakers.

Only those who punish lovingly punish justly.

LAYMEN

We are all laymen, only some more so than others.

LEARNING

It is the learned who forever threaten the peace of man—not the illiterates, but the Rameses, the Attilas, Caesars, Hitlers, Stalins. Whatever they and their entourage lacked, it was not learning.

❦❦❦

Learning of the brain will further the ability to create new appliances for human comfort—but what of human peace?

❦❦❦

Speak to your own self and let it teach you.

❦❦❦

Honor is a poor reward for the pleasures of study. Where honor is set as the price of education, the mind may pack in many facts and data in its hasty reach for the goal, but the heart will become forbidding and corrupted.

❦❦❦

Education must serve a purpose or it may fall into a wrong one. Tradition had a grip on the school as a parcel of princely property, and to use such property on behalf of the crown was the scope of tradition. Such scope is unchanged in the lands which are vassals to totalitarian masters, where the youth is no more than a chunk of state property manipulated, like all of life, limb and holdings, for the benefit of a demagogic clique. But in the free lands, youth is not a means but a goal, each person to be respected as a body and mind in his own right, to be dealt with not in competition and tasteless comparison.

In our free society we aim to treat the porter with the same regard as the pundit, the janitor like the judge, the pauper like the millionaire. Upon such equality our social organization is based, and in such equality our youth is to be raised. The poor in memory, the poor in perception, the slow in thinking and the weak in diligence are to be handled with the very same attitude as those enriched in all respects.

A child can as little help being lesser mentally as it can help being so physically. There is as little fairness in catering to the

[83]

gifted and setting back the deprived as there is in constantly praising the beauties of a pretty child and noting the defects, scars and pimples of a homely one.

LEISURE

People go to great length to get their working time reduced; then they take this hard-won time—and kill it.

❦❦

Leisure is the dream-time of doing nothing spun by the many who stay on the wrong job.

❦❦

The great hunt of the masses: to kill time.

LIE

Some would search and twist to come to truth, while others do the same to protect a lie.

LIFE

Is a rather short walk through eternity. Be they seeds, pups or infants, on the trek all pick up weight, sensitivity and awareness. Then, much before the end of the run, they deteriorate, head, legs and lungs. The tragicomedy of existence: the long walk of slow decay.

❦❦

It is not how old you are that matters, but how many hours of your life you have lived.

❦❦

Man creative lives many lives; some men are so dull they do not live even once.

❦❦

Life is so crowded with everyday, it takes great effort to step aside and just watch and think.

❦❦

Few only live their own life; so many have it lived by others.

❦❦

[84]

Many are so preoccupied preparing themselves for life that when they are about ready, it has already passed them by.

❧❧

Life is a process of dying, from the breaking of the first membrane to cessation of a complete organism.

LIFE SPAN

It is less important to extend life in length than in depth.

LISTENING

Many words remain unspoken when men are deeply moved and only those who listen with the inner ear can hear them.

❧❧

The most precious thing a man can lend is his ears.

LITERACY

Has not abolished the world's grievous problems, wars and tyranny, but it has made a greater number victims of them.

LITERATURE

Most books aren't worth the eye-strain.

❧❧

There are confidence men in literature as well as in finance, business and politics.

❧❧

The worst thing that ever happened to writing is that it became a business. The purpose of business is to make money, and to achieve that end it is necessary to please as many people as possible, to amuse them, to entertain them—in short, to do everything that will help increase the volume of sales.

❧❧

A book occurs when man experiences things of great depth and significance and feels compelled to relate his inner experiences. There are such books, written ones as well as unwritten ones.

❧❧

[85]

If only those would write who have something to say, many who should only watch would get off the field.

LIVE
As you want to be remembered.

LONELINESS
Even the gods would be lonely without man's myrrh and liturgy.

❧❧

Loneliness is rare and peculiar company.

LONGEVITY
Even the fleeting butterfly has an infancy, adolescence, middle age and senescence. Perhaps a select few live a bit beyond their three score and ten hours.

LOVE
In love as in religion only those who share the little rituals stay together.

❧❧

If only man would stop loving humanity and deity and begin to love just himself—not that in himself which is on the lowest level of man, but rather that in himself which occupies the highest rung.

❧❧

The word "love" belongs in that small group of general terms that is used more frequently to disguise an intent or a thought than to divulge it. And if "love" is used in combination with "humanity," the word becomes the most dangerous befogger of them all.

❧❧

To love people is to know them.

❧❧

There is a lover even for a crab.

❧❧

Love is the passion of grief. Amid all the sunlight of affection, there falls the shadow of life rushing away.

❧❧

All men love themselves, but some also hate the rest of the world.

❧❧

Hate comes naturally, love is to be learned.

❧❧

Love may be so ethereal that the presence of the beloved may reduce the state rather than increase it. Still, love is no more than the wish to be together.

Love is the desire to be together, and no more. Whoever sends his beloved away has long ceased to love, no matter how reluctant he may be to admit it. Sometimes nostalgic tremors may linger on after the beat of love has been stilled.

❧❧

There are some words that need to be broken up, such as "love." There should be different terms for the lust to mate and for man's heartful devotion to kin, friend or God.

When Messalina seduced a new slave into her bedroom, she called it love; when King David heard of the death of Jonathan, he cried out, "I loved thee more than this earth understands"; when a lecherous roué marries his latest child-bride, he quakes, "I love you"; when the prophet Isaiah fell under the dagger of the assassin, he is said to have shouted, "Jerusalem, I love thee!"

If love is of Isaiah, it fits not Messalina. It is a poor banner indeed that serves the knight and the highwayman, and if it stands for crime and seduction, it does not grace issues sanctified by supreme devotion, loyalty, kinship and sacrifice.

❧❧

No one can love his enemies unless he first makes them his friends.

LOVERS

In history tell not of the nights but the days of love.

LOYALTY

To trust the erring is generous, to trust the disloyal is weakness.

❦❦

To hear some talk, one might think that disloyalty is a privilege and not a villainy.

LUST

Is lust and has its place, but not as a metaphysics.

LYING

May not be good, but the bare truth is not always a blessing.

M

MACHINE AGE
It has enlarged the possibility of tyranny from a local matter to intercontinental scope.

MALEVOLENCE
Rides easily on the tongue; it is the good word that sets heavily in the throat.

MALICE
Is not innate but inbred.

MAN
Some love nature to the exclusion of man, but he is one of God's creatures, too.

※※

Men are petrified children. If one would only try to visualize them as they were when children, one's understanding would be easier and one's judgment kindlier.

MANNERS
Man's toilette manners have improved, his church attitudes hardly changed.

※※

Good manners may require restriction of conversation to pleasantries, but, then again, good manners will not improve the world.

MARRIAGE
Is the only business in which adolescents are permitted to make a contract.

Marriages may be made in heaven, but people live on earth.

MARXISM
Created dictatorship over the proletariat, not by the proletariat.

MARXIST ATHENA
The Pharaohs of yore claimed descent from the gods: those of today stoutly maintain they sprang directly from the head of Karl Marx.

MASSES
No man is so small that he does not consider himself above the masses.

They say the masses need religion; rather the power-mad leaders need it and need it badly.

The masses are not those who think but don't know; rather are they those who know but don't think.

MATERIALISM
I suspect the enemies of materialism. They either live off idealism or drape it about themselves like a cloak to keep from being touched by the tears and sweat of the victims of ideologies.

MATHEMATICS
Is the language through which nature speaks to her children —but there is also God, and He is not a mathematician.

MEDALS
The noncombatant invariably winds up with the largest string of ribbons and medals.

MEDICAL FALLACIES

There is hardly a medical fallacy that was not at one time or another "standard treatment." Who knows which of our present "standard treatments" will be the fallacies of tomorrow?

MEMORY

To remember the correct date is a gift; to remember the correct principle is a virtue.

The power of remembering may be a gift, but the power to forget is a blessing.

Why retain a mental picture of trifles? Only great events are worth remembering.

MERCY

Words of mercy are a bow toward Heaven but deeds of mercy open its gate.

Mercy is thrice justice.

MIDRASH

Or the oral interpretation of the Bible has about run its full course and exhausted every possible aspect. We need less exegesis and more emphasis on the true principles of the Old Testament, which can be reduced to a one-page fundamental.

MIND

A glass splinter reflecting a ray of infinite Sun, dreaming of itself as hearth of the universe.

Mind is an open garden and weeds are plentiful.

Too much emphasis is given to the mentally deviated and not enough to the mentally corrupted. It is not the neurotics who retard the world's progress, but the ruthlessly ambitious.

There are some ill-fitting gears in the mental machinery. To most questions we seem to find, or hope for, a corresponding answer, yet there are queries open that foil even an attempt to reply.

❧❧

Mind mirrors reality, or only glows like a window reflecting a distant ray—who can fathom this phantom looking glass?

❧❧

Mind measures the vastness of galaxies, visible and supposed, and finds it cannot sustain the vision of endless firmament. Endless space and infinite time are just the whisper of a bewildered soul.

❧❧

If God is anywhere, He dwells within that heart of hearts raising its eyes to the infinite. God finds Himself in the mind of man; the mind's vision of God is God Himself.

MINDS

On guard for the little falsehood often fall prey to the big one.

MINORITY

The student of history knows that the minority has, often as not, been closer to the truth than the dominant group.

❧❧

A minority has no right to govern, but a claim to be respected.

MIRACLE

Nothing seems to the masses more plausible than the improbable.

They will readily accept a fantastic wonder of the past but, for the present, they will have no miracles.

❧❧

Miracles are no proof of saintliness. The Devil performs them too.

[92]

MIRROR

Every once in a while we stop and quickly glance at our friend to find out how we look in his eyes. The rest of the world matters little—it is how our friend reflects our deed that counts. We all live lonely lives except for that mirror.

MISERY

Can live without company but joy cannot.

MISMANAGEMENT

Openly acknowledged is a sign of democracy; in tyrannies there *seems* to be always perfection.

A MOB

Has many heads, but most often only one cunning brain doing its scheming.

MODERNISM

Is the belittlement of a splendored past by a dull present.

MONASTICISM

One does not get closer to God by leaving the world. The Shepherd can best be found near to His flock.

MONEY

Some honor what they lack more than those who possess it.

MONUMENTS

Should be erected to the great evildoers. It is more important to keep them fresh in the public memory than the benefactors.

❦❦

Fortunate for us that the hallowed statues of some exalted personages cannot come to life again.

MORALITY

Is a set of rules that all men are breaking day in, day out—only some rather noisily.

❦❦

Morality is certainly wanting in some respects, but immorality is a poor substitute.

Morality is the observance of the rights of others. One cannot be immoral but in relation to others. What one does to oneself or with oneself may be wise or foolish, but never immoral.

One may abuse his body and yet be respectful of the welfare of others and thus quite moral. And one may discipline his flesh with all precepts of hygiene and asceticism and be a hard, selfish, hurtful person and thus grossly immoral.

It is only in relation to society that man is good or bad, moral or immoral. By himself he may be sober and moderate or very careless, but never good or bad.

I do not think that abstinence is a way to morality, but goodness is.

Morality is always the same. However, immorality varies from generation to generation.

Nothing is immoral that is not meant to hurt others, and nothing is moral that is meant to do so.

MORTALITY
Is a sobering thought. Unfortunately, it occurs to most people at a time when it is too late to do anything about their lives.

MOTIVES
Hold the reins over man's mind.

MOURNING
Dead heroes will not bring them back, but fulfillment of their plans will give them eternal life.

MUSIC
The wordless cry of the inner soul reaching for love's fulfillment and beatitude. Beethoven's symphonies, the slow move-

ments: The Lord Himself walks through the silent forests of His domain.

There is another music: the stirring beats of lusty savages, the screech and fury of bored sophisticates jazzing a tired night to death, the whinny of the devil on the brink of borderline humanity.

❧❧

I have often wondered why men write music to poetry and rarely poetry to music. It would be a great and new art to set the symphonies of Beethoven into poetry!

N

NAMES

Should be assumed, not presumed. The Jews, for instance, were given offensive names by some of their presumptuous Christian neighbors in order to embarrass them.

Names should be changed to suit men. Some trail ludicrous appendages after them. I have seen giants with names suitable for a dwarf and women with men's names.

Names should be means of identification and decoration, not embarrassment and confusion.

NASTINESS

Is the tyranny of the peewee.

NATIONALISM

It is peculiar that nationalistic zealots are not even natives of the countries they allegedly wish to glorify: Alexander was not a Greek, Napoleon not a Frenchman, Hitler not a German, and Stalin not a Russian.

NATURAL LAW

Man is inclined to elevate his hypothetical explanations of natural phenomena to the status of Universal Laws.

THE NATURALIST
Touches the hem of God and he thinks he feels the pulse of the Lord.

NATURE
Who can fathom why nature is so designed that creatures can exist only by destroying other creatures?

❧❧

Nature, never wrong, wrongs many.

NEGRO
Someday a lotion may solve an issue where emotion has failed; a yet-to-be-found chemical will neutralize the dark pigment of our neighbors and leave the many palefaced inferiority complexes stranded on their prejudices.

NEGRO BAITERS
They call on Jesus in the church and on Beelzebub in the street.

NEIGHBORS
One always carries their picture with him, but often it is a caricature.

❧❧

Do not bother loving them—just cease hating them.

NEUROTICS
Leave them with us! They are the spice in our bland diet! Leave us Dostoyevski, Paganini, Beethoven! Take not from us the impulsive, faddish, and fantastic, the romantic and illumined poets, the prophets and arty princes lest we remain a race of ordinated zeroes led by rosy-cheeked dullards out of a well-adjusted textbook.

❧❧

The American society is hard on the hunt for neurotics, but the great evils in the world are perpetrated by the so-called normals, not the deviates.

[97]

In Russia, sober, calculating politicians are keeping millions in concentration camps and are giving a deadly time to their Jewish citizens, for instance, simply in an opportunistic speculation of gaining power in Western Asia. In Red China scores of educators and jurists, following a peculiar brand of socialism, advise the young on how to denounce their parents who do not follow the official party line. Such denunciations invariably end with the elders being publicly executed before the very eyes of grisly, elated, icy youth.

And in our lands, cold-eyed townsmen of the South refuse to convict perpetrators of murder and kidnaping on blacks, while unemotional, shrewd legislators of the White Council stamp rant against basic principles of humanity.

All these and many other sinister elements in our society are the drags that stop humanity from rising to loftier heights, not the unimportant neurotics screwed up in their petty little complexes.

NEUTRALISM

In the fight between the red and the black, some prefer to remain colorless. If you look hard you may note the yellow showing through.

NEW ERA

A new epoch began with the Nuclear Terror overhanging. We have left the era of incessant wars and entered the period of peaceful animosity.

NEWS

Is not what you read today but what happened today.

NIGHT

Is perhaps a reminder to us that our globe orbits in the dark of space.

NOBILITY

The psychoanalyst wants you to do the smart thing, God wants you to do the noble thing. Where do you wish to make your place, on the couch or in history?

Nimbus rises not from a callused palm or a belabored brain, but from a gentle heart.

O

OATH
The offhand remark of an honest man is better than the oath of a weakling.

OBEDIENCE
To the rule of the tyrant is nothing but rationalization by the moral slave.

OBLIVION
Is not the enemy of the great; rather do their false and fanciful disciples place them in the shade.

OBSCURITY
Scratch the obscure and you find a simple man.

OLD AGE
Stars that have been ignored all morning, noon and evening open up in the late of the night to brighten the hours of the lonely wakeful.

＞＜＞＜

As you get closer to the end, the "big things" of life lose their size and the little things loom bigger and bigger.

＞＜＞＜

Happy the man who gains sagacity in youth, but thrice happy he who retains the fervor of youth in age.

OPINION

The great obstacle to truth is the common man's lethargic reluctance to make a thorough house-cleaning of his mind.

OPPORTUNISM

There are two ways of looking at the world and there are two ways of leading one's life: to do what is right, or to do what is opportune. By this proposition there are two types of persons, opportunists and the right kind.

How many rush to the support of the strong when the weak are in distress!

OPTIMISM

Is a devil-may-care hope born out of the fear to face hard truths.

Optimism may change your mood, but nothing else.

Optimism can be a matter of philosophy as well as disposition.

ORATOR

Being great in rhetoric without profound calling or message is like being adept in stage fencing—without purpose or honor to the rapier.

ORATORY

The magic quality of making a trickle thunder like a torrent.

ORTHODOXY

No one is more insufferable on rigidity of observance than the man who has nothing else.

Orthodoxy with many is purely pretentious or nostalgic, like the meat-eater belonging to a vegetarian society.

[101]

OTHERS

What makes you think you look better to others than they look to you?

OUR WORLD

God is in His heaven and the Devil on earth.

OVERLORDSHIP

Was once established by the strong fist, then by the keen blade, and now by the sharp tongue.

P

PAIN
Pain is always a fanged serpent, but to the fearful it has a hundred heads.

PARADISE
Is nowhere, but peace can be had anywhere.

PASSING
You shall not live your years again, so treasure them hour by hour.

PASSION
Is given to prophets as well as to sinners.

Passion is no sin; history is alive with dispassionate enemies of humanity.

PAST
Our known past is but a brief paragraph in the book of time.

PATIENCE
Is out of place in the quicksand.

PATRIOTISM
So many of the great patriots were and are men of age. Men whose lives are flowing away caress the beloved nation of which

they are a part. It is in the love of his people that mortal man never dies.

☙☙

Patriotism is too often not an attitude but a profession.

☙☙

The patriot is not the one who loudly praises his own; he is just a braggart. A patriot is the man who praises the land and the people that are dedicated to freedom and brotherhood.

PEACE

Loud talk about an allegedly desired peace is a common device to disarm the victim before attack.

☙☙

The Caesars were in the habit of vehemently pleading for peace whenever they planned an attack against a quiet neighbor.

☙☙

Peace is possible only when the law is greater than men. The tragic situation is that in most lands there are still people who are greater than the law.

☙☙

Submission to tyrants makes not for peace but unending war.

☙☙

Peace with the Devil remains a one-sided arrangement.

☙☙

Even an angel could not live in sanctity with the Devil about.

☙☙

The people of today are as peaceful as they ever will be, but still there are hangmen at the helm of state. The warmongers of our time do not thunder from shaggy horses—they are doctors of philosophy like Mao, theologians like Stalin, schoolteachers like Mussolini, painters like Hitler, or jolly organizers like Khrushchev. But they have bled to death more men and women than the malefactors of all the past generations put together.

PEDAGOGY

Went a-traveling to many far places, but bloodshed remained at home—fat, red, ugly as ever.

PENS

Too many push a pen who should wield a broom.

PEOPLE

Whoever loves not his people, loves not God. The Lord made the covenant with a nation, not an individual.

Perhaps the people are as gullible as the charlatans seem to prove.

You can't remake all people, but you can manage to avoid some of them.

The voice of the people is seldom their own.

PERCEPTION

Of all new people, events and ideas takes place on the used film of our brain; even a brand-new picture registered by our mind is distorted or blurred by the thousand faded prints already on our memory.

We cannot hear the thunder of the galaxies churning through endless space, nor the whisper of the neutrons colliding in the atom world; there is so very little our ears can register or our eyes behold.

PERFECTION

The perfect man is not one without faults, rather, one burdened with all sins and blessed with the will to overcome them.

To the ant, its hill may be a perfect world; to the rest, it's just another bit of sod.

PERSUASION

Is a privilege of democracy and the weapon of tyranny.

PESSIMISM
Consoles itself with inevitable sorrow even as optimism with its inevitable joy, and the rest of the world may whistle for its salvation.

❦❦

Pessimism is the twin sister of optimism, fleeing into the bleak vastnesses of the mind in head-over-heels flight from the field of action.

PETS
So long as there is a suffering waif starving in this bitter world it is a sin to cater to a dog.

PHILANTHROPY
Is no evidence of faith, but indifference is proof of itself.

❦❦

Watching public benefactors is an embarrassment to the indifferent; they will steadfastly belittle the motives of the donors, having themselves no motive at all.

PHILISTINES
They give such little answers to such big questions.

PHILOSOPHERS
Are amazed at what most people take for granted.

❦❦

The world is full of peacock philosophers who forever are preoccupied with their own feathers.

❦❦

Philosophers and opossums have the habit of looking occasionally at the world upside down. It is a surprising experience.

PHILOSOPHY
Is a queen in exile, having lost her entourage but not her regal demeanor, hoping that someday her prodigal servants will return disillusioned with themselves.

❦❦

Hesitancy is the beginning of philosophy, and charity its end.

꧁꧂

It is the ability to hesitate before forming an opinion that makes the difference between a philosopher and, shall we say, a parroty mind. Snap judgments are like fishing nets cast with great flourish and prematurely hauled in. A lot of seaweed and broken shell may come up, but hardly any fish.

꧁꧂

Philosophy is either a way of life or a mere figure of speech.

꧁꧂

Philosophy deals with man, not books.

꧁꧂

Philosophy can never be defined because it is the search for the indefinable.

꧁꧂

All man's world is in man's mind; mind's mind *is* man's world.

To the timeless universe coursing through infinite space, what is all this but the dreams and doodlings of a blade of grass in the evening wind?

That which man calls "beauty"—what is it? That which man calls "moral"—what is it? What he calls "heritage"—what is it? The blade of grass is singing in the wind and it thinks the wide, wide universe hearkens.

Still man must live as if his world were real and perennial, but if he finds his true and tiny measure, a better man he may be— more humble, more kind, more forgiving, more hesitant.

꧁꧂

Philosophy is the Cinderella of the sciences; she does not even possess her own definition. But once in a generation or so the fairy prince gallops up and raises her high to the castle in the sky.

꧁꧂

Philosophy like all true friends will show up best in times of adversity.

[107]

PIETY
The heartbeats of the Lord are a pulse of harmony, a pulse of love. Are you listening?

PITY
Is where man meets God in fellow man.

PLEASANT
There is nothing more irritating than unpleasant things said in a pleasant manner.

PLEASURES
Can be found where you least expect them.

❦❦

There can be as much joy in helping along as in tripping up.

POETRY
What enchanting webs of sentiment are spun by the poets about such trivial props as the moon (a bit of burned out stone), the clouds (a loose volume of steam) and the blossoms (leaflets decaying above the sprouts of some weed).

❦❦

Poetry: Language of the wounded soul.

❦❦

Whispering melody from the faraway shores of man's pained soul, true poetry is ever melancholy. Plato named it a mania. Is that why every fifth one of the great bards lived or died in broken mind?

❦❦

Poetic license does not extend to politics.

❦❦

The court poet may ride a gilded charger but never Pegasus.

POLITICIANS
Live off the people, statesmen for them.

❦❦

[108]

Politicians are never more dangerous than when they discover in themselves love for mankind.

POLITICS
A profession holding out the greatest amount of power for the least amount of training or responsibility.

POSTERITY
May also err, and its mistakes are difficult for us to correct.

POTENTATES
The world has always had those who take on the voice of God, and sound off for themselves—those with the cunning tongues who, in depicting the Lord's celestial abode, never fail to point out their own right of eminent domain in its anteroom.

POVERTY
Is the disgraceful symptom of our whole known era, that forever wastes the people's sweat on the mansions of the rulers, cheapens the price of blood in defense of them, and raises the cost of bread for the expendables.

Only the freedom of tears exists among the masses of Eurasia and Africa. And the princes of Arabia or India, the chieftains of Russia or China, may toss a fortune into armlets or arms while the people perish in want of nourishment.

❧❧

Poverty is a disgrace, a disgrace to human fellowship.

POWER
Still comes first in Eurasia's nations, with scholarship a stumbling, rationalizing second. After the ugly deed is done, theory is called in to contrive justification.

❧❧

Power is what they seek, the ambitious beetle, ant, or spider —until a careless step by some wandering animal crushes their flimsy web or nest.

[109]

PRAISE

Watch out for praise; its twin is derision.

PRAYER

Where the heart does not long for love eternal and peace among men there is no communication with the Divine; there is no true prayer. Prayer is the pining of the soul of man for the soul eternal, in this aimlessly drifting world of evil and illness, pain and deceit.

❦❦❦

Those who pray to God for blessings beggar the grace of worship.

❦❦❦

A serene word, a chapel on your lips, if those lips were only for fellow man and fellowship instead of for favors and privileges.

❦❦❦

With the slaughter, in less than a decade, of every third Jew by the German people, in the souls of worshiping Jews Divine Providence receded into the background. The mood of the synagogal worshiper changed from the prayerful to the meditative. Judaism, especially Reform Judaism, shifted to a philosophical vein: God no longer the benevolent Father, but *ens perfectissimum*, the light of cosmic cognition, *Or Adonai*.

❦❦❦

The Lord knows your needs, what wants revealing are your deeds.

❦❦❦

Pray to your conscience for guidance and not to the Lord for deliverance.

PREACHING

Is like delivering an ambassadorial message: it is the King's voice that should prevail and not the messenger's fancy.

[110]

PREJUDICE

There is no smugger contentment than being safely surrounded by one's prejudices.

Logic is ever so often the handmaiden of prejudice.

Nothing is better established than prejudice, hatefulness and superstition, and nothing sounds more convincing than an old lie.

The prejudiced will only know what his fellow man lacks, not what he possesses.

Superstitions and prejudices of distant lands and times are readily apparent. It is those close by that are difficult to discern.

Prejudices cling most readily to the very young and the very old.

Prejudices seem to have some sort of birthright in the mind: they are there before enlightenment.

THE PRESS

Should be free but not loose.

PRIDE

Is a virtue if it is the measure of one's own nobility. It renders itself a sin when its intent is to make others appear ignoble.

PRISONS

There must be a better way of re-educating offenders than herding them like unruly cattle into a pen.

PROGRESS

Mankind's speed has quickened but our track is still the very same circle.

In the last hundred years we have been going two steps forward and three steps backward.

❧❧

Tribes used to call each other by beating on tree trunks, then by scratching on clay tablets and paper, and now via electrons.

Still, after thousands and thousands of years, the text of the messages has not changed: tribe trafficking with tribe to destroy other tribes.

PROOF

You can't prove anything where interest dominates reason.

PROPERTY

Because fortune attaches itself to a man does not make him a fortune hunter.

THE PROPHET

Knows no more than ordinary man but he knows it earlier.

❧❧

Very few, blessed few, pin their faith directly on the word of God. Most ordinary people anchor their beliefs in other mortals who link God to them. The Hebrews called these prophets *nebiim*, "interpreters."

PROSPERITY

Is as often the midwife of generosity as of arrogance.

PROVERBS

Much cherished wisdom of Western philosophers was, millennia before, folk wisdom in other continents.

❧❧

Proverbs are the mirror of a people. If we read the proverbs of the Sumerians or Israelites, ancient as the sands of the desert, we begin to realize how little we have added in all the thousands of years to their wisdom of life.

PROVIDENCE

Is childishly anthropocentric wish-thinking that the Winds will change course to blow a dust particle off a petal.

THE PRUDE

Is closer to sin than the indifferent; in fact, the former is ever on the brink of it.

PRUDENCE

May fill the purse but empty the heart.

PSYCHOANALYSIS

Hanging a Greek tag on every quiver of human emotion may create the illusion of knowledge where there is only classification.

~~~

Psychoanalysis: The attempt to cure aberrations of the present day by recalling aberrations of the past.

~~~

Mind bespeaks itself. One who finds his milieu a forest of sexual symbols reveals more the status of his own brain than that of his environs.

~~~

Psychoanalysis has added many new words to our language but no new insights.

~~~

Dreams are the play of a drowsy mind; only fools and children take a game for real.

PSYCHOSOMATICS

Many illnesses originate in the mind; the body lives correspondingly. The problem is: which came first, the inside of the shell or the outside?

PUNISHMENT

Habitual criminals should be punished with compulsory labor which they dread far more than compulsory idleness.

~~~

Punishment is not the answer to the problems of crime; it answers only the call for revenge.

[113]

Q

QUESTIONS

A thousand questions can be posed off the beaten path; even correct replies will lead nowhere.

R

THE RABBI

Speaks of the Sages and the Sages speak of God. You cannot place a statue on the bare ground, you need a pedestal. The rabbis are the pedestal. It is a thankless lot to have chosen. They serve to enhance the greatness of the Masters and the best they get is to be overlooked.

RACE

God cannot see the marks and markings by which humans distinguish themselves from others. He can but see the humans.

❦❦❦

A thousand things distinguish man from man, but only one distinguishes man before God—his conscience.

❦❦❦

Little people make much of the little which makes them different from another, but to the aeons eternalizing the universe, man differs from man as barely as a dust grain varies from a dust grain.

❦❦❦

How little do we know of man's past and how much do we make of that little we know.

❦❦❦

Race is good when taken as an obligation, evil when taken as a privilege.

❦❦

If each race were human, there would be only one.

REASON

If man be rational then I don't know the meaning of reason.

❦❦

The semblance of reason is often more attractive than reason itself.

REBUTTAL

Silence is the argument of the sage.

RECLUSE

To make nothing of the world will not enrich the Heavens and leave the world as poor as ever.

REFORM

Is seldom effective without a dose of reaction.

REGRET

Redress is needed, not regret.

REINCARNATION

May be true, but I do hope that some who have passed away never come back again in any shape or form.

RELIGION

Not all religions are good, but there is good in all religions.

❦❦

Man's religion is accidental but his faith is not.

❦❦

Perhaps all of it can be defined in the admonition to offer your fellow man the first cut of bread.

REMORSE

Is the gate to ethics, but will carry one no further.

REPOSE

Is not the absence of tumult but mastery of it.

REPROOF

Is only welcome if its aim is to raise up, not mark down.

REPUTATION

Is not worth defending, but righteousness is.

〜〜

Reputations often travel in opposite directions from their subjects.

RESIGNATION

Perhaps the wisest begin and end their lives in obscurity, and even in passing, steal away from the rest without an epitaph—unknown giants in a realm of dwarfs.

RESURRECTION

The breathtaking concept of man's religion, an immortal soul in eternity!—in small eyes, a selfish vision of personal reward in a comfortable hereafter arranged by a police-judge type deity for the goody-goodies.

RETIREMENT

Assigning a man a deathbed as his future living quarters.

RETRIBUTION

Is not God's way, but man's wish.

REVENGE

Uses the words of justice but the voice is crime's.

REVERENCE

Those who have no regard for their own dignity will never cherish it in others.

REVIEWERS

Some forget that they are only heralds and not the heroes of the play.

REWARD

Education won for a reward is like love won for a bracelet.

RIGHT

May not always make might, but you'll not find it while on your knees.

❦❦

The test of existing rights lies in daily practice, not in abstract constitutions.

RIGHTEOUSNESS

It is never too late to start on the path of righteousness, and the road to evil will always be only a step away.

RIVALRY

The common habit of "encouraging" students by public shame and public prizes to push themselves to the front benches may improve their marks but mark them for life.

❦❦

Rivalry is the root of all social evil—and yet it is nurtured still in our pedagogy.

❦❦

The wish to outdo others is a greed, not a virtue.

ROMANCE

Lives not in the people but in their dreams. Who does not dream will never encounter the greatness of love, daring, adventure and devotion.

ROYALTY

Somewhere on every royal coat of arms should be engraved an executioner's ax.

❦❦

Royalty used to carry a scepter, now it sports a vodka bottle.

RUSSIA

The land where the accused knows the verdict before the jury.

⚜⚜

The Soviets have all but conquered illiteracy, yet in the excitement of the campaign they mislaid The Book.

S

SABBATH
Is not sanctified by abstention from work, but rather by devotional attention.

❧❦❧

God gave you six days, give Him one!

SALVATION
To many, Jesus is an alibi not a savior.

❧❦❧

Socrates has no followers because his testament was that salvation must be earned by every man for himself. Jesus' flock runs into millions because He took the pains of salvation upon Himself.

SANCTITY OF LIFE
Is a great principle to uphold but greater yet is that of the dignity of man.

❧❦❧

Sanctity of life is a noble but inconsequential attitude. The ankle bell of the Hindu, which sends out warning to whatever crawls of the crushing threat of his feet, sounds gentle enough, but besides the millions of ticks and worms that draw their life from the skin and blood of man, there are billions of minutely tiny beasts infesting man's arteries and tissues that must be poisoned so man may live. Holy only is the life of no sin; much of the animal life that crawls and flies is a curse to man and a disease.

[120]

SCHOOL

Youth has a right to be regarded as a goal and not as a means. In free society every boy and girl has a right to live a young life of self-respect and respect without comparison to others, be they better or worse, more clever and adept or less cunning and diligent. If a teacher cannot deal with the young but by the whip of threats and the bribe of rewards, he is as little fit to sit under the blackboard as a judge with such a frame of mind would be fit to sit on the bench.

Every boy and girl has a right to have his or her natural gifts of body and mind tended to, be they great or small, as individual talents, without being driven to demoralizing contests for scholastic rewards, without being subjected to the dehumanizing effects of shabby victories over classmates and equally dehumanizing humiliation of alleged failure. It is easy to deal with pupils, whip in one hand and honey in the other. Labor used to be dealt with in the very same way, but the time has come to drop the sorry tradition of competitive schooling as the time came generations ago to drop the tradition of competitive labor management.

The praise and rewarding of the gifted and diligent is as demoralizing as the public criticism of the less endowed and less patient, because the goal of education does not lie in the subject, but rather in the student. It isn't what you put in the student that matters so much as what you bring out of him. You may pour into his brain with Nuremberg funnel all the seven wisdoms, up to the rim; if you can't get out of him the spark of human kindness and the yearning to raise the standards of mankind in a life of co-operation, you may have gained him a whole array of honors and medals, but you have rendered no service to youth and society.

❦❦

School is the place where family prejudices are replaced by public ones.

SCIENCE

Has brought little peace on earth or to the soul of man, although it has brought many comforts to body and business.

❦❦

Excepting medicine, science has enhanced our lives with little comfort that wasn't thrice outweighed by bloody damage, be it by powder, plane or atom.

❦❦

Some fight religion in the name of science; on closer inspection, both seem to have eluded them.

❦❦

Man's ax got sharper, not his wit.

❦❦

Knowledge makes man neither free nor good. The Romans, most learned of ancient peoples, tolerated Caligula and Nero, and enthusiastically carried the scourge of the Fasces into peaceful neighboring lands. The Germans, most learned of the twentieth century, elected a paranoiac housepainter as chancellor and tumbled gleefully from executions to death-camps and back.

Knowledge and science are tools that can be used for evil as readily as for the good. The scientist or scholar is not made a better man by his knowledge, only a more dangerous one.

❦❦

Perhaps science has harnessed enough of the powers of nature; let us now harness the powers of science.

❦❦

Science began with a gadget and a trick. The gadget was the wheel; the trick was fire. We have come a long way from the two-wheel cart to the round-the-world transport plane, or from the sparking flint to man-made nuclear fission. Yet I wonder whether the inhabitants of Hiroshima were more aware of the evolution of science than ancient man facing an on-storming battle chariot.

It isn't physics that will make this a better life, nor chemistry, nor sociology. Physics may be used to atom-bomb a nation and chemistry may be used to poison a city and sociology has been used to drive people and classes against classes. Science is only an instrument, no more than stick or fire or water that can be used to lean on or light or refresh, and also can be used to flail or burn or drown. Knowledge without morals is a beast on the loose.

❦❦

Science is hidden behind a tight web. Every so often someone unravels a tiny thread, getting a glimpse into her mysteries. A thousand riddles are still far away from our peepholes.

❦❦

They teach what science has accomplished. They need to tell also, and more so, the unfinished business of science, the long index of matters unknown and problems unsolved.

❦❦

In their rush for new comforts and expediency scientists have left man's peace of mind where it was when they started three hundred years ago.

SCIENTIST
Seems to be a title reserved not for the philosophers and those who study human nature, conduct, ethics, history and faith—but solely for those who work in rocket fuel, atomic fission and plastics.

SCRIPTURE
Some swear by God's scripture but act by the Devil's script.

SECOND CHILDHOOD
The old seem to be in second childhood because they have learned that much of life is better taken as a game than a gauntlet.

SECURITY
Is a blessing, but not if bought at the expense of fellow man.

SELF-CONFIDENCE
Does not always bring a man to the top, but no one ever got there without it.

[123]

SELF-ESTEEM
Think of yourself as you wish others to think of you.

SELF-GOVERNMENT
Perhaps some of the less modern nations do not yet know how to govern themselves, but their colonial masters have certainly proven they cannot do it for them.

SELF-IMPROVEMENT
There is no short cut to self-improvement away from the main road of world betterment.

Self-improvement is a meaningless effort. The Self is God-given and wants no betterment. The task is to reach one's Self and to be true to it conscientiously.

SELFISHNESS
All men are selfish, but how their selves differ!

Selfishness is a commendable instinct, if man would only find his true self.

SELF-KNOWLEDGE
Everyone knows himself best, but refuses to admit it for fear of incrimination.

SENSE OF HUMOR
To laugh at oneself is both wit and wisdom.

SERENITY
Those who have not found a spiritual harbor in which to anchor their thoughts find themselves adrift at every squall.

Serenity is as often the result of indifference as it is the sequel to philosophy.

SERMON

The flocks should leave impressed by the Lord, not by the Rabbi.

SERVILITY

Is a form of inverted arrogance.

❧❧

Those who bow to the man above will invariably step on the man below.

SEX

Was always here but never so much talked about.

❧❧

If it were man's dominant motive, then the peasant who conducts his sex life on the level of stable husbandry could be considered its best-adjusted master.

SHREWDNESS

Experience makes for shrewdness; it's the heart that makes for wisdom.

SICKNESS

Some suffer more from their remedies than their illnesses.

SILENCE

May be golden, but sometimes it is only yellow.

❧❧

Silence is the voice of the convinced; loudness is the voice of those who want to convince themselves.

❧❧

It is not the stillness of the tongue that matters but the silence of the heart.

❧❧

Silence is the gate to understanding.

SIMPLICITY

The truly wise are always simple. It is the little mind that spins complications.

❦❦

Simplicity is the garb of wisdom.

SIN

Is sweet. Were it not, it would not be necessary to prohibit it.

❦❦

Sin is the weak man's failing, the strong man's secret.

❦❦

A man's omissions are the measure of his deeds.

SINNERS

Lead an interesting life but wind up with loss of their capital.

SKEPTICISM

Be quick to doubt and you hasten reason.

❦❦

Skepticism is only an approach to sagacity, not wisdom itself.

SKY

Is just an ocean of gases in which trillions of minute creatures are floating; they swarm around the tasty globe like gnats around a cut fruit, these ubiquitous tiny beasts, infecting man, animal and plant.

SLAVERY

It is shocking that the two philosophers who dominated the Western mind for two thousand years, Plato and Aristotle, upheld slavery as a God-given institution.

Slavery was certainly not born with Plato and Aristotle. But their books justified, to an adulating Europe of so-called Christian faith, the idea that some were born free and some born slaves.

The fantastic situation lies in the utter indifference of the Christian world to the obvious contradictions existing between the teachings of Christ about the equality of men and the preva-

[126]

lent enslavement of serfs, bondsmen, and kidnaped blacks by Christians.

The freeing of slaves, tragically enough, was not done by, but in spite of, the Church.

The slave's chains are still there; yesterday, about his neck; today, about his mind.

SLEEP

Is a refueling process of body and mind. Sleepers' chill is indicative of the great energies used in this process. Perhaps some day a way will be found to replace the natural manner of slumber's revitalization by speedy chemical means. The Man of Tomorrow may not sleep at all.

Perhaps it is Sleep that, in replenishing the body energies, saps our strength. Is that why they call him the brother of Death?

Sleep is the harborer of dreams as heaven of the stars; but who pays heed to gazers at the both?

SMILE

A smile is still the best make-up for a face.

The flag of truce in a world of strife.

The manner of wisdom.

Smile! If only for the lift it gives your company.

Smiles will turn no torrent nor smooth a tempest into zephyr, but they make the journey so much pleasanter.

SNOBBERY

Is an attitude of infantile forgetfulness—forgetfulness that in this fleeting ocean of life all these man-made distinctions born of petty desire, created by smallish minds, are mere pebbles over which the water-mountains float endlessly, majestically.

❦❦

You can't pull rank on God. No man walks past Saint Peter's gate with a monocle in his face.

SOCIALISM

The blueprint of paradise over a foundation of purgatory.

❦❦

A government of the many at the mercy of a few.

❦❦

The shamefaced cousin of Communism, losing virtue by kinship rather than misdeed.

SOCIETY

The clue to a man's true nature is the character of his enemies.

SOLIPSISM

Perhaps the whole wide world is only in our mind. In that case, let's have an orderly mind!

SOLITUDE

Is a state of mind, not a geographic position. There are no lonelier places than certain spots in certain crowds.

❦❦

Solitude: alone with a throng of phantoms and the kaleidoscope of imagination.

SOPHISTICATE

A person who derides all standards in order to avoid the job of studying them.

❦❦

Wisdom by necessity will "no" some things and "yes" others; the frivolous steal the nimbus of wisdom by deriding all and sundry.

SOPHISTICATION

Cracking a thought into a joke.

SORROW

Is the messenger of friendship.

SOUL

Souls must lead a harrowed life within the stormy body-complex of cells and blood and nerves.

❦❦

It takes all the skill of steady husbandry to raise a soul to bloom; most of them lead a stunted existence and wilt before their petals open up.

SOUL-DOCTORS

Help should be given to those who deserve it, not those who can afford it.

❦❦

So many search the souls of others who have yet to look into their own.

SPACE TRAVEL

We are morally in no better position attempting to visit other planets than the murderous goldhunters Cortez and Pizarro. We are a nefarious lot with a record of twenty million killings in the last few decades alone. What have we to offer? A globe that has not learned in a million years to govern itself and still feels ready to strike out for new territory.

SPEECH

Don't judge a man until you have heard him speak. The voice is the truest mirror of mind and intent.

❦❦

Speech is called the mirror of thought—perhaps that's why so many ideas appear concave or convex.

[129]

SPIRIT

Is the spice of life. It is *Shekhinah*, the Hebrew for the living God. Of course one can live a whole existence on a spiceless diet.

STAFF OF LIFE

A man's soul feeds on either love or hate. Some live on the pleasures of the good deed; others are of such disposition that only doing hurt and harm will nourish them. Ormuzd and Ahriman, Moses and Pharaoh. . . .

So many live on a diet of hate, cherishing envy and greed like satiating herbs, while love is shunned like a poison. These cannibals of the soul have infested the caves, tents and roofs of all the continents. They have made man cry out in anguish of war and torment since the birth of Adam.

But somehow there always rose those who would bear the symbols of the Lord and stretch out their arms in beatitude.

STATESMAN

The path of the statesman is haunted by politicians—starlings in the flight of the eagle.

⁂

Statesmen see themselves as handmaidens of history; politicians see the state as a handmaiden of themselves.

STATUES

There are too many on horseback. I would like to see more standing on the sod, at the lathe or beside a desk.

STUPIDITY

Is sometimes more of a defense than a characteristic.

STYLE

Some persons forgot to put on this season's opinions and now everybody thinks they are old-fashioned.

⁂

Mind makes the style, not vice versa.

[130]

SUBHUMAN

Some are wisened by human affairs, others by subhuman.

SUCCESS

I know of no greater failure than the man who devotes his life to the achievement of success.

❧❧

The man who sets success as his goal is doomed to failure, since one desire for achievement succeeds another in the endless chain of human vanity.

❧❧

Fancy props don't make up for a shoddy play.

SUFFERING

Will hearten some and harden others.

SUICIDE

To die at one's own hand may be of more grace than living in subjugation or disease.

❧❧

There is a commandment "Thou shalt not kill," but none "Thou shalt not die."

THE SUN

It is not earth that is mother of man, but the sun. The sun gives its nourishing rays to the plants, which man and his animal-food live on; the sun evaporates the water that filters into man's springs; the sun warms the air man breathes and the ground he walks on. Man is truly a child of the sun. Still, whence does Helion draw its matter and energy? Wherefrom the unknown and perhaps peregrine donor?

❧❧

The energies that carry this our globe and billions like it through space and time are breath-taking. And this is but the tiny universe that our tiny cornea envisions.

What mysterious other attributes must that Unknown Eternal possess that we call with the ancient nomen: God. Perhaps the Hebrews were right in warning: Name it naught but the Eternal, the One.

The Sun is what you make it—the Light of Lights or just an extension of bursting gases.

SUPERIORITY

There are no people with a superiority feeling, only those with an uncontrolled desire to hide their inferiority.

SUPERSTITION

Is the anteroom to religion where those remain who cannot get an audience with their own selves.

SUSPICION

May as well be the gate to knowledge as to hate.

SUTTEE

The now obsolete Hindu practice of burning widows exemplifies the petrification of moral principles. In earlier scriptures of Hinduism there is a solemn plea for connubial devotion beyond the grave.

SYMBOLS

Words are only symbols; if those who argue only realized how little they differed in facts!

SYMPATHY

Arguments may win the day but sympathy will win the man.

T

TALE

Truth is so hard to tell, it sometimes needs fiction to make it plausible.

TALK

Deep-bottomed boats travel slowly.

❧❧

Talk is primarily a way of killing time. Perhaps that explains its popularity.

❧❧

Mankind divides itself into two types: dialogue people and monologue people. The latter never hear you or your side since they are pauseless monologists.

❧❧

A peasant may be more interesting than a scholar if the peasant opens his soul and the scholar only an odd book.

❧❧

Though you don't hear the fish, it doesn't mean they are not talking.

❧❧

Some talk of a thousand different things and still speak only about themselves.

[133]

TASTE

Is the feeler of man's appetite and still the best judge of right nutrition.

❦❦

Taste is spoiled in childhood by parental prejudice and in adults by customs and fads.

TEARS

Come readily from shallow souls.

❦❦

Blessed the tears shed for the brother's woe and the smile over the neighbor's happiness!

TELEOLOGY

If man is nature's ultimate goal then this is an awfully small world.

❦❦

Man is as little the final purpose of divine providence as an elk or a beetle or a salamander.

❦❦

Teleology in its attempt to find a man-suiting purpose in nature will have to contend with the teleology of plants, animals and perhaps other entities.

Were the sunflowers placed in the meadow as supply source for the bees; or as food for some parasites; or for man to look at; or to drop to the ground and serve as fertilizer for surrounding weeds?

What a tragicomic pose! Tiny man no bigger than a mold traveling on a gigantic rock through billions of years and miles in an unfathomed galaxy of innumerable worlds, yet hollering at the top of his inaudible voice: Hear me, trillions of universes, aeons of times, infinities of space! I, man, earthbound fungus, 98 per cent water, 2 per cent phosphor and such, I am the aim and end of it all. I am the purpose of all this majestic movement in its mysterious history!

Perhaps the Torah was right in forbidding man to set himself in stone or paint, lest he feel himself lasting or even everlasting. Is he more than a pinch of dust with a whisper of breath?

≈≈≈

If there be purpose to this world in its crazy meandering, it can't be a good one. By all human reckoning there is more sin harvested in a day than goodness planted in a year.

TEMPER

Let your thoughts be burning, but your words cool.

≈≈≈

Watch your voice and you need not watch your words.

TEMPTATION

The Devil just testing.

≈≈≈

It is easy to resist the big ones; the little ones cause havoc.

THEODICY

Not all is good and beautiful in this world, but then neither are we.

≈≈≈

We find a spider web glistening in the morning dew enchantingly aesthetic—yet it is only the shroud of a still-kicking victim. The nightingale breaks into a delightful cadence of song whenever her golden throat swallows the crushed worm; and who has not admired the picture of leonine majesty resting satiated in the bush, a limp half-eaten doe under his mighty paw. The world seems ordained to mutual destruction in a chain of necessities.

THINKING

Thought is a twig on the tree of emotion and instinct. As it was a million years ago, the first is still an outgrowth of the latter.

≈≈≈

Men think quite alike; if it were different, they could not coexist even for a day. But most people judge by traditional or imitated judgment patterns, and snap judgments are the rule and the rulers.

❧❧

Is thinking ever free? Wherever I meet it, I find it chained to a *motive* of one kind or another. The world operates on motivated thinking tied to prejudice, opportunism, greed, narrow-mindedness, selfishness, and a thousand other little passions and passionettes that clutter up the narrow path of righteousness.

❧❧

Thinking can be shaped by heart, gall, glands, stomach, or even shifting eyes. Sometimes I wish that people's thoughts came in colors so one could see what part of the body sent them forth.

❧❧

Thinking may be classified on a color chart, however, of poetic imagination. Some people's cogitations run rosy; others gray, even black. There are those who think yellow and those who live and breathe blood red. The minds of others are of peculiar color combinations. And there are sages whose badge is white, embodying all the colors. No human emotion is strange to them, yet none colors their thoughts.

❧❧

A good thought, even when poorly presented, will finally emerge right side up.

❧❧

The last thought is always wiser than the first.

TIME

Time does not heal wounds, it just hides some and deepens others.

❧❧

How quickly does today turn into yesterday.

❧❧

Time took the wrong road. The Past was not all glory; there was wilderness. But now we are trapped in a Death Valley with no sight of a Tomorrow.

❧❧

No one can plot the path of time; perhaps we have been standing on a byway for centuries, thinking our dead end was the summit of it all.

TIME AND SPACE

Live on borrowed existence: they are not really there, they just relate to each other.

TODAY

Is to be lived as if it were tomorrow, because tomorrow is only belated yesterday.

TOLERANCE

Must stop at the threshold of monstrosity.

✷✷

Tolerance appears in two editions, one bound in wisdom and one in indifference.

✷✷

Tolerance is ill used on friends of the great sinners. When the sinners fall, some of their friends plead the thin excuse of compulsion. The sycophants are always ready to serve the new master and renounce the old, but the Hebrews said you cannot be Abaddon, angel of the bottomless pit, and Gabriel in one person.

TOMBSTONE

Better study your epitaph now lest your tombstone belie its dead.

TOMORROW

If a tomorrow were never to come, it would not be worth living today.

TONGUE

The tongue is man's best friend but also his worst enemy.

✷✷

The pen may be mightier than the sword, but mightier yet is the tongue. The tongue-waggers are the masters of our era, the Hitlers, the Stalins, the Mussolinis. The swish of their tongues is deadlier than all weapons.

❦

Buddhists attribute four evils to the tongue—slander, lying, idle talk and offensive speech—and only three to the rest of the body. By their words you shall judge them. Vicious tongues have incited to world-wide massacre and have ever so much prejudiced thinking among men and nations, races and creeds.

TORTURE

Nature is beset with suffering, but of all beasts, only man makes a business of prolonging it.

TOTALITARIANISM

This granite earth we live on could be a bed of roses were it not for the scheming Procrustes and his fellow henchmen, be their shirts black, brown or red.

❦

The Red camarilla has taken the romance out of socialism and replaced it with opportunistic expediency, thus losing the best of the idea and acquiring the worst that is in imperialist government.

TRAINING

You cannot train a horse with shouts and expect it to obey a whisper.

TRAVEL

People travel to faraway places to watch, in fascination, the kind of people they ignore at home.

TREASON

Once a traitor, always a question mark.

THE TREE

Is the symbol of wisdom: it never shouts, and only whispers when it's moved.

TRITE

We call the oft-repeated truism which we have accepted for the record but never for real—for example, Love thy neighbor.

TRUST

Is an expectation based more on the hopes of the person having it than on the nature of the one trusted. No one is so deceitful that he has not been trusted by some and sundry.

TRUTH

To judge truth by its expediency is like calculating the profits of love.

All men can savor truth, but it has to be served differently from one to another.

How come the sages of all times speak the same truth? The Hebrews revere *Shalshelet Ha Cabbalah*, the Chain of Tradition. There is a chain of tradition running from the days of Ur to our time, but familiarity with the so-oft-repeated pronouncements of the prophets has estranged us. Perhaps the sayings of our fathers should be translated into a foreign idiom and then brought back as a rare find, in order to be listened to again!

Man's mind is confounded by the deceitful twins: hearsay and gainsay.

Truth drops its wings before a low-ceilinged mind.

Truth hurts only the liar.

Truth may not make you free but falsehood will enslave you.

People spend more time on camouflaging truth than in uncovering it.

TYRANNY

Is tyranny, no matter what banner is flown from the halberd.

U

UGLINESS

Little uglinesses fill the air of our society like insects. They don't kill you, but they make life miserable.

Ugly faces suffer little temptation.

UMBILICAL CORD

The invisible tie between the young and their parents that seems to be blissfully light when the traffic of benefits goes child-ways, but tautens to unbearable pressure when the young are called upon to share responsibilities and let the advantages flow the other way.

UNCONSCIOUS

Man is pretty well aware of which currents course through his gray matter; he conceals them so well, however, that it is his neighbor who remains unconscious of their existence.

Man is an open book, but he does not care to have you read over his shoulder.

UNDERSTANDING

Exists on infinite levels. A moth comprehends the candle light, so do a dog and a bird; an infant figures it out, so do savage and savant. There are infinite attributes to all manifestations of the universe and endless variations of conception.

❧❧

It matters little whether people misunderstand you, as long as you don't misunderstand them.

UNIONISM
In the political and social fields runs smoothly uphill from the individuals to the centralized top. From there on, the chances are, star persuaders will drag the whole lot into a downhill alley of their own ambitions.

UNIVERSE
To find order in the cosmos is fundamental, but beyond our concept of the universe looms a greater one.

❧❧

Man resides on his little globe like a coral in a tiny, lost pool; the great waves of the mother ocean hardly ever reach his shores.

❧❧

We know there are rhythms in the cosmos but who keeps the beat and what is the score?

❧❧

There is more mystery in the yolk of an egg than in a galaxy of planets, if we could only fathom it.

❧❧

Universe is only the little cosmos we see with eye and telescope. Beyond the beyond is *Pantaverse*, the endless worlds of worlds—*Ain Soph*, the Cabbalists named it, the One Without End.

UNPLEASANTNESS
With some, it is just a way of giving themselves airs.

UTOPIA
No promise or hope of tomorrow's better world is worth the price of today's liberty.

[141]

V

VALOR

Is a matter of the mind. It is in the choice of purpose that valor differs from recklessness.

❧❧

Valor is measured by the height of the cause not the heat of the battle.

VANITAS

If only the conquerers realized in time that their deeds are a game with worthless chips. After taking all the mountains and seas, they wind up like everybody else with a muddy slab of stone and their name on it.

VANITY

Can work through a display of poverty as well as through a show of wealth.

❧❧

Vanity has no greater offender than the one who flaunts his indifference.

❧❧

Vanity is no sin, resignation no virtue; ascetics have lit fagots under fellow creatures and dandies have fallen in defense of the innocent.

[142]

VEGETARIANS
Like the whale, they prefer flesh of the invisible animals to that of the visible ones.

VICE
Is a sickness rather than a sin; not the dissipating but the malevolent are damned.

VIRTUE
Carries its own reward. Were this not so, only the superstitious would pretend to seek it, anticipating post mortem advantages. But true virtue, as well as true knowledge, is flavored by that rare beatitude called by the Hebrews *Simcha Shel Mitzwah*, "the pleasure of the right."

Beware the one whose virtue lies in the fear of God and not in the love of man.

All sins are common to all people, but virtue is of the few.

Virtue lies not in kindness, but in constant kindness; even beasts commit single acts of generosity.

Virtue is the strength to do good in the face of evil.

VISION
Some are so nearsighted they only see themselves.

VOICES
Rise and cease, yet the voice of silence speaks forever.

W

WAR

Living in appeasement under a dictator's yoke has all the sanguinary possibilities of war without the chance of redemption by battle.

War is not in the nature of man; defense is.

As far as the people themselves are concerned, they have little or nothing to gain by war, but everything—including their lives—to lose. In this sense, war is not in the nature of man, only in the nature of tyranny.

Wars of independence are but the inverted will for peace.

Perhaps the coming wars will be fought with pens instead of swords. The sting of the pen may be no less sharp than that of the edged weapon.

Little men who want to be remembered start great wars; great men who wish to be forgotten are the architects of peace.

Wars have changed their weapons but not their retribution.

[144]

WEAKNESS

Is often goodness ill-received.

❦❦

We see nothing clearer in others than our own weaknesses.

WEALTH

Is no crime and poverty no virtue. Many who champion the cause of the poor live more like those they attack than those they defend.

❦❦

Wealth of nations should be measured not only by the economy of material goods, but also by the resources in mind and heart. How poverty-stricken some of them are in their richness!

❦❦

Wealth does not preclude virtue and poverty does not imply it.

WICKEDNESS

Harbors often within those you least suspect.

WILL

Riding the unbridled steed of passion thinks itself the master of the reins.

❦❦

Will is awareness of a desire with a set of motivations more presupposed than comprehended.

WILL POWER

A tiny fraction only of man's actions are known to him. The thrust of the pulse, the rushing of the blood in a thousand veins and arteries, the flow of a hundred springs in glands and tissues, the chemical reactions in the transforming mechanisms of stomach, kidney, spleen and gall, the lighting of impulses in brain and nerve cells—a billion molecules within the framework of Homo sapiens are acting out a miniature universe, infested always by

[145]

enemy microbes demolishing the very foundations of this thing called man.

Man's will controls only a minute fraction of the powers that move him.

WISDOM

There is a lot of foolishness in the wise and a lot of wisdom in the foolish.

Like victory, wisdom lies in the final outcome, not in the individual contest.

WISHING

Is the hurdle on the track of thinking.

WIT

May appear without wisdom; wisdom is never without wit.

WOMAN

Is not an equal but rather a sequel to man.

WOMEN

So often confuse poseurs with pioneers. The retinue of most charlatans is nine women to one man, and about this one I am not always sure.

Women are the bearers of culture but not its makers. They read philosophy but do not write it, play music but do not compose it, view art and architecture but do not create it.

WORDS

Spoken by sect-ridden prophets and class-strugglers have done more to divide people than issues or things themselves.

Words offer a mine of information for those who dig deep enough.

WORK

The lowliest job can be made interesting and the most exalted become a bore.

❧❧

Work is man's most natural form of relaxation.

WORLD

A chimaeric scheme of interconnecting gears made up of living creatures who can exist only by devouring each other.

WORLD GOVERNMENT

Is wonderful; but first, where is that world?

WORSHIP

Is either Judaic or Pagan, philosophical or idolatrous. The Hebrews worship no man, no saint, no priest, no face—only the *Echod*, the One, *Ain Soph*, the Infinite, *Elohim*, the Eternal.

The pagan, whatever his denomination, wants a man-god, a visible, walking, talking and personal god or goddess. He believes not in the invisible, he yearns for ikon and amulet, flesh and blood. But stone and flesh and blood and gold cannot fit the heart of man to the *Or Adonai*, the light of the Lord, in which we see Him with our love and conscience, in deeds of justice and charity; which deeds are the Alpha and Omega of true faith.

❧❧

Be familiar with the Lord. Invite Him as often to your house as you visit His.

WRITERS

Are moved too much by the expectations of their public, rather than by their own momentum.

WRITING

Whoever writes with ease carries little weight.

❧❧

So many with nothing to say keep on saying it.

☙☙

Good writing is simple writing. Only confusion is complicated, truth never.

WRONGS

Were we to remember all wrongs done to us, we would live forever in hate.

☙☙

A wrong forgotten is a wrong set right.

Y

YES!

Is the first word from the lips of the Lord, No! the first from the mouth of the Devil.

YOUTH

Is not indicative of progress, nor age of reaction.

☙☙☙

Youth is only the beginning of old age.

☙☙☙

Youth comes many times if the mind is kept aflow.

☙☙☙

Nothing is more conducive to a youthful old age than a serene youth.

☙☙☙

Youth may spot the failings of the old but often misses their virtues.

☙☙☙

What impressed us long ago may have left our minds, but the impression has not.

☙☙☙

It is better to die young than to live old.

☙☙☙

Every age has its own beatitudes; those of youth can never be repeated although they are never forgotten.

Z

ZEAL

The Lord is not in want of zealots, but of souls.

ZEN

There are many shades of darkness, but only one principle of light. The experience of *Satori*, the enlightenment of Zen; the meditation into *Samahadi* of the Hindus; the *Tao* of Lao-tse, the road to inner self—they all are only different symbols signifying the Hebraic *Or Adonai*, the light of God which Spinoza so beautifully named *Amor Dei Intellectualis*.

ZERO

They say that if all living humanity were placed body to body, they would fit into a cube no more than one mile in each dimension. One short mile out of the tens of thousands that make up this globe that, in turn, is just one battered rock out of billions of the kind we can see by eye and instrument.

Were one to visualize this one cubic mile of Homo sapiens sunk into a canyon or crater, what becomes of the world and worlds? The blades of grass would rise green as ever, the waves of the seven seas would storm and heave, the lava never cease its flow in the volcano and the starry skies not even blink at the anthill of humans, all gone out at once instead of in bunches.

That cubic mile of man is destined for burial in some canyon or crater, all two and a half billion segments of it, within a few fleeting decades, but, dropping to the ground, they leave their offspring for a like existence of passing fortune, which gives them the feeling of perennial life.

If all people were to be buried on one day and in one casket, instead of in billions of small interments, perhaps that thought would make them realize how much like planetary dust their life, how ludicrous their arrogant distinctions of race, class and what they call religion, which means "binding," but with most of them serves rather to separate than unite.

Perhaps the day will come when this planetary dust that grew into flesh only to find its way back into a dugout of dust again, when this man of clay will truly reach awareness of his pitiful frailty and prove by deeds of charity and loving wisdom that somewhere, somehow in this mysterious universe there is a flame of godliness burning in aeonic distances and that a spark of this fire shimmers in the soul of man.

There is so little that we know even of what we can see about, beneath and above us, and what we can see is but a speck of the *Ain Soph*, the Endless, of which we can only dream in faint concepts.

Man's inhumanity to man has left its sanguinary mark upon the earth and waters of this globe since the days of earliest recollection. Forever some cunning creature would rise in piracy upon his neighbors and sway his tribe to carry out a nefarious scheme of pillage, rape and conquest.

If only those strutting evil little masters of some anthill of land would understand that with all their bluster, medals and fanfare, they, too, are only clay on clay, and the dust of their graves is no respecter of tinsel and rank; and if the many who follow their power-usurpers on the bloody path of tyranny, if they, too, would learn it is better to lead a simple life on your feet than a fancy one on your knees.

If they would only understand that the pleasures of humiliating others and holding neighbors in chains are as fleeting as the dust in the wind—and that is all man is, dust in the wind of time.

If they would only understand that there is a serenity of the soul which comes with the practice of kindness to man, a serenity which outlasts the winds of time, since it is born in the heart of hearts, where dwells the insight into the majestic unity of this our universe.

You may call this God, or the voice of God; we Hebrews call it *Echod*, *Adonai*, *Elohim*, the One, the Lord, the Eternal.

Give it the name you will, this nameless One, but let your deeds be in His grace and His charity.